## GCSE ENGLISH LITERATURE

# Students' Book

*Jackie Bivens*    *Tony Farrell*
*David Stone*

AQA ENGLISH LITERATURE
SPECIFICATION B

**OXFORD**
UNIVERSITY PRESS

# OXFORD
UNIVERSITY PRESS

Great Clarendon Street, Oxford OX2 6DP

Oxford University Press is a department of the University of Oxford.
It furthers the University's objective of excellence in research,
scholarship, and education by publishing worldwide in

Oxford  New York

Auckland  Bangkok  Buenos Aires  Cape Town  Chennai
Dar es Salaam  Delhi  Hong Kong  Istanbul  Karachi  Kolkata
Kuala Lumpur  Madrid  Melbourne  Mexico City  Mumbai  Nairobi
São Paulo  Shanghai  Taipei  Tokyo  Toronto

Oxford is a registered trade mark of Oxford University Press
in the UK and in certain other countries

British Library Cataloguing in Publication Data

Data available

ISBN 0 19 831896 0

10 9 8 7 6 5 4 3 2 1

Printed in Italy by Rotolito Lombarda

# CONTENTS

**Acknowledgements**

The article by William Golding published in *The Daily Mail* 17.02.93 reprinted by permission of Faber & Faber on behalf of the estate of William Golding.


**Photo acknowledgements**

AA World Travel Library: p 97 (bottom); Alamy: p 88; British Film Institute: p 18;  Charles E Brock: pp 116, 118; Corbis: pp 110, 133, 136; W Cody/Corbis: p 56;  Chinch Gryniewicz/Corbis: p 108; John Heseltine/Corbis: p 87; Military Picture Library/Corbis: p 141; Gail Mooney/Corbis: p 81; Alastair Shay/Papilio/Corbis: p 121 (bottom); Frank Ward/Corbis: p 85; Terry Whittaker/FLPA/Corbis: p 62; Corel Professional Photos: pp 16, 33, 43, 77, 127, 134, 135; Digital Vision: Title page, p 74; Eyewire: p 52;Hulton Getty: pp 7; 14 (top), 22, 38, 41, 60 (both), 121 (top); Illustrated London News: pp 4, 14 (bottom);  23 (all); Michael Mayhew: p 25;  The National Trust Photographic Library: p 97 (top); PA Photos: p 67;  Photodisc: p 91,  99, 125, 138; Susan Scott: 48;


Cover photographs by Digital Vision (background); Alamy (bottom); British Film Institute (middle bottom); Corbis (top) and Corel Professional Photos (top middle).

# ABOUT THIS BOOK

Working through this book will help you to read, understand, and enjoy plays, poems, and novels – and carefully prepare you for your Literature examination.

The book is divided into three section: Drama, Poetry, and Prose, which is the order in which they appear in the English Literature examination. Each section has a short introduction written by a senior examiner, followed by closely detailed work on specific texts. The sections are also divided into pre- and post-1914 works.

The first section is on **Drama**. It features detailed work on *The Importance of Being Earnest* followed by two post-1914 plays, *An Inspector Calls* and *Pygmalion*. There are sections on the **social, cultural, and historical context** of the plays and their **literary tradition** – two important features of the drama questions in the written examination – and on the plays' **plots and structure**. The plays' **themes and issues** are discussed, and there are sections on **characters** and **language**. Throughout, activities will help you get to grips with the main ideas you will need in the examination.

For **Poetry**, there are four units all looking in detail at poems in the *Best Words* selection: two units look at poems from the pre-1914 period, and two look at the more modern poems from post-1914. The pre-1914 poems selected are: *To Autumn, Amen, First Love, To His Coy Mistress, The Flea, Ballad, Porphyria's Lover,* and *My Last Duchess*. The post-1914 poems are *An Advancement of Learning, Churning Day, Roe-Deer, Mirror, Long Distance, Afternoons, My Grandmother,* and *The Sick Equation*. The guidance given will ensure that in the written examination you will be able to compare two poems successfully, and to write about the ideas in the poems and the way the writer has used 'the best words in the best order'. The aspects considered include **subject matter, themes, language,** and how to approach **comparison**.

The final part of the book looks at **Prose**, with the following novels closely analysed: *Wuthering Heights, Far From the Madding Crowd,* and *Pride and Prejudice* from pre-1914, and *Of Mice and Men* and *Lord of the Flies* from post-1914. Again there will be sections that help you with the novels' **background, plot, characters, language,** and **themes**.

Because the help and advice in this book is written entirely by experienced examiners, you can be sure that they know the best way to prepare you for your English Literature examination. If you follow their advice carefully, you will ensure that the quality of your answers improves, resulting in higher grades. Enjoy your reading!

# INTRODUCTION TO DRAMA

This section of the book will help you to study the play you are reading for your end-of-course examination, so that, when the time comes, you can feel confident that you know the play and could tackle any question.

## WHAT WILL THE EXAMINERS EXPECT OF ME?

First of all, whether you are studying a pre-1914 or a post-1914 play, you need to demonstrate your **knowledge** of the play – what happens and to whom, who does what, where, why, etc. However, this does not mean examiners want you to summarize the plot – believe it or not, they have read the plays and have probably seen them performed more than once! They want you to use your knowledge *selectively*, to pick out relevant aspects that will help you answer the question.

This means that you must focus closely on the question. Identify the **key words**, keep them at the front of your mind, and refer to them regularly.

## WHAT KNOWLEDGE AND UNDERSTANDING DO I NEED?

It is important that you show you understand the **background** and **context** of the play.

- What was society like when the play was written?
- What attitudes and beliefs did people have?
- What about the playwright? What sort of life did he or she lead?
- What attitudes and beliefs did the playwright have?
- How do these contribute to the message of the play?

You will find several **research activities** in the following units. These are designed to help you find out about these social and contextual issues, so that you can understand what the playwright was trying to get across to the audience. Once you understand something about the society and attitudes surrounding the writing of the play, you will find it easier to get to grips with what the playwright was trying to say about contemporary life.

It is also important that you understand the **generic features** of the play. Remember that plays are written to be performed on stage in front of a live audience, not to be read. This obviously has an effect on structure, action, and interaction. Information has to be given through dialogue and what the audience can see on stage, unlike in a novel, where there is the opportunity for description and narrative. So you need to be aware of any descriptions the playwright gives of the settings or characters. Pay attention to the stage directions, particularly when they instruct the actor how to speak – 'angrily' or 'reproachfully', for example – or how to move (such as 'purposefully'), or to look ('astonished'). Try to be aware of what these directions suggest in terms of personality, action, behaviour, and underlying theme. The stage directions tell the actors how to behave in order to convey the message.

Obviously, you need to have some idea about the **themes** or the main messages of the play.

- Why was it written?
- What was the playwright trying to get across to the audience?
- Did the writer just want to entertain them or to make them think?
- If so, to think about what?

You also need to be aware of the more obvious aspects of any play, and you are bound to discuss these things in class. Clearly, you must be able to write about the **characters** – who they are, what they do, how they behave and respond to others, how they interact, how they change – everything about them. Also, the **structure** of a play is important – when and why scenes and acts end at specific moments – does this create tension? **Dramatic tension** is important – plays do not work without it, so look at what is happening when the curtain falls or the scene changes, and ask yourself why.

**Remember:** Always look carefully at the examination question – what are the key words? Focus on these, and write about what you are asked to write about – **answer the question!** Then you will be showing your knowledge and understanding of all the above features in ways that will gain you the most marks.

# THE IMPORTANCE OF BEING EARNEST
## Oscar Wilde

*Before beginning this unit, go back to pages 2–3 and read again what examiners are looking for in an essay about pre-1914 drama.*

## BACKGROUND AND CONTEXT

Oscar Wilde was born in Ireland in 1854, the son of a distinguished eye surgeon. He studied at Dublin University and then Oxford, where his flamboyant personality and behaviour attracted much attention.

Wilde's writing was amazingly versatile. A volume of poetry was published in 1884. He wrote several fairy stories for children (including *The Happy Prince*), as well as the Gothic melodrama *The Picture of Dorian Gray*, and several plays, including *Lady Windermere's Fan* and, in 1895, the highly successful play *The Importance of Being Earnest*.

Soon after the opening performance of *The Importance of Being Earnest*, Wilde was imprisoned for homosexual activities. After his release two years later, he moved to France where he died, bankrupt and broken.

### RESEARCH ACTIVITY

Wilde led an exciting and colourful life. Investigate some aspects of this. You could consider:

◆ his fairy stories
◆ the effect of his disagreement with the Marquis of Queensberry
◆ his life at Oxford
◆ the story behind *The Picture of Dorian Gray*.

Before his imprisonment, Wilde moved in influential circles, being accepted as a member of high society. This element of Victorian society tended to be pompous, considering itself to be extremely moral and serious. It was also very superficial – trivial matters were often treated more seriously than important issues. In *The Importance of Being Earnest* Wilde makes fun of this; the title informs us that the play is about being *earnest* or serious. Wilde is also using a pun – it is important to Cecily and Gwendolen to marry men called Ernest!

1   The play is both a **satire** and a **farce**. Investigate the meanings of these terms and compare your findings with others in your group. You may find more recent and famous examples of both satire and farce. What would you say are the key elements of farce?

2   The play contains examples of **paradox, reversal, epigram**, and **puns**. Find out what these terms mean and be ready to spot examples.

## PLOT

The basic plot of the play is quite straightforward.

Jack Worthing, who also calls himself Ernest, is in love with Gwendolen Fairfax. Her mother, Lady Bracknell, questions him about his background to assess his suitability as a husband for her daughter. She discovers that, as a baby, he was left in a handbag at Victoria Station, and was subsequently brought up by Mr Thomas Cardew, who made Jack the guardian of his granddaughter Cecily.

Jack's friend (and Gwendolen's cousin) Algernon pretends to be Jack's brother Ernest. He meets and falls in love with Cecily Cardew.

Both women insist that they can only marry someone called Ernest. This presents the men with the same dilemma and they both consider being re-christened by Dr Chasuble.

Lady Bracknell recognizes Cecily's governess, Miss Prism, as the person who disappeared some years previously with Lady Bracknell's baby nephew. Jack is therefore Lady Bracknell's nephew and Algernon's elder brother. He was christened Ernest, so he does not need to be re-christened. He and Gwendolen will live happily ever after, as will Algernon and Cecily, and Miss Prism and Dr Chasuble.

**WRITING ACTIVITY**

Find out the meaning of the following terms: *guardian, ward, governess, christening.*

## ACT 1

Act 1 is set in the 'lavishly and artistically furnished' London flat of Algernon Moncrieff, who is awaiting the arrival of his aunt, Lady Bracknell. The opening exchange between Algernon and his butler, Lane, sets the tone for the rest of the play. Lane's first words foreshadow the numerous jokes that make fun of upper-class society – the people, their attitudes, and their way of life.

Notice how the conversation moves between serious and trivial matters, from the science of life to cucumber sandwiches, to champagne, to servants and masters, to marriage, and so on.

> ▌**WRITING ACTIVITY**
>
> As you read through Act 1, map the topics mentioned under the headings **Serious** and **Trivial**. You could present this in the form of a spider diagram.

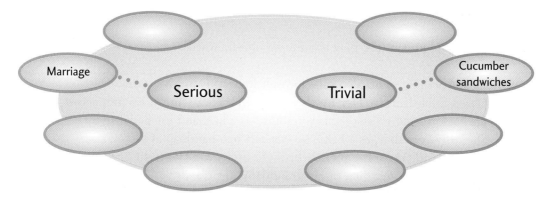

Algernon's friend Jack Worthing arrives and explains his intention of proposing to Gwendolen Fairfax – Lady Bracknell's daughter. A great deal of the comedy hinges on the idea of his double identity and his non-existent brother, Ernest. Jack claims to be visiting Ernest whenever he comes to London. He is considering 'killing off' his brother because his ward, Cecily Cardew, is too interested in meeting him. If Gwendolen accepts his proposal, there will be another good reason for getting rid of the imaginary brother. Algernon reveals that he has an imaginary friend – Bunbury – whom he claims is ill whenever he wants to get away from London.

> ▌**WRITING ACTIVITIES**
>
> Look closely at the opening scene before the arrival of Lady Bracknell.
> 1   What information have you gained about Algernon's way of life? What evidence is there to support your findings?
> 2   Explain how this opening section introduces the theme of lies and deception.
> 3   Which comments do you find to be the most funny? Explain your choice of at least **six** quotations.
> 4   These opening moments give early examples of the way in which Wilde **reverses** well-known sayings or beliefs; for example, the reference to the lower orders reverses the Victorians' belief that it was the responsibility of the upper classes to set an example. Find other instances of such reversals as you read through the play. Explain how they work, and comment on their comic effect.

Lady Bracknell arrives with her daughter Gwendolen. Lady Bracknell and Algernon go out to discuss the music for a reception on Saturday, leaving Jack (Ernest) and Gwendolen alone. He almost reveals his true name, but she declares that she could only love someone called Ernest. When Lady Bracknell re-enters, Gwendolen tells her mother about the engagement. Lady Bracknell questions Jack to find out if he is suitable.

## WRITING ACTIVITIES

5   Look at Lady Bracknell's interrogation of Jack. List all the questions she asks and her responses to his answers. What is her final piece of advice to him? What comment is Wilde making about people like Lady Bracknell and their lifestyle and attitudes?

Jack tells Algernon he intends to 'kill off' his imaginary brother, and they consider how Cecily might react. Algernon says he would like to meet her, but Jack is protective of her. When Gwendolen returns, Algernon eavesdrops on their conversation and discovers Jack's country address.

### RESEARCH ACTIVITY

This act contains numerous references to fashionable places such as 'Half Moon Street' and 'Willis's'. Find these and other references, and research some information about them. What do these references tell us about the way of life of the upper classes?

Add information to your chart of 'serious' and 'trivial' references.

### ESSAY QUESTION: ACT 1

Act 1 closes with the following words:
**Jack:** Oh, that's nonsense, Algy. You never talk anything but nonsense.
**Algernon:** Nobody ever does.
To what extent do you agree that the characters in Act 1 talk nothing but nonsense?

## ACT 2

The setting moves to the garden of Jack's country home. Cecily Cardew, his ward, talks to her governess, Miss Prism, about Jack and his 'brother', who has apparently been very wicked. They discuss fiction, and Miss Prism reveals she once wrote a three-volume novel, but lost the manuscript.

When the vicar Dr Chasuble appears, Cecily persuades him to take Miss Prism for a walk to ease her (non-existent) headache. Merriman, the butler, announces the arrival of Ernest Worthing, and Algernon enters. He claims not to be as wicked as portrayed, and flirts with Cecily as they move into the house. When Miss Prism and Dr Chasuble return, their conversation is noticeably more serious and academic. Wilde is deliberately presenting us with a contrast.

**WRITING ACTIVITIES**

6  Investigate the following references:
   ♦ Mudie and the three-volume novel
   ♦ Egeria
   ♦ Don Quixote.
7  Explain the significance of the arrival of 'Ernest Worthing' in the light of what you know of him. How might this add to the comedy?

Jack appears, dressed in mourning clothes, and announces the death of his brother in Paris, where he is to be buried. The audience knows that 'Ernest', or Algernon, is in the house with Cecily. Jack asks Dr Chasuble about being christened, and agrees to 'trot' along that evening.

Cecily appears and tells them of Ernest's arrival. Cecily persuades Jack to shake hands with his 'brother'. Jack is keen to get rid of Algernon, who is equally keen to stay and has come prepared to stay a week.

Alone with Cecily, Algernon (Ernest) admits that he has fallen in love with her. She produces 'evidence' from her diary to show that they have been engaged for three months! She also explains that she had always dreamt of marrying someone called Ernest, thus placing Algernon in the same situation as Jack. He goes to find Dr Chasuble.

**WRITING ACTIVITIES**

8  Explain how the theme of lies and deception has been developed so far in this act.
9  Many serious aspects of life are trivialized here. Examine the way the characters talk about and react to education, death, christenings, and engagement.

Merriman announces the arrival of Gwendolen, who has come to visit Mr Worthing – she thinks he is Ernest, but the audience knows him to be Jack Worthing. Cecily invites Gwendolen into the garden and asks Merriman to serve tea. Cecily explains that she is Mr Worthing's ward. Their conversation reveals that they both think they are engaged to Ernest Worthing. Jack is Cecily's guardian, but Gwendolen has known him only as Ernest.

Both women produce diary entries to prove their position as Ernest Worthing's fiancée. The tone of their conversation changes from friendly to frosty. They remain polite in front of the butler but begin to insult each other more when he has left the room.

## WRITING ACTIVITIES

10   In what ways is Gwendolen like her mother?
11   Comment on the epigrams in the women's conversations. Consider, for example, the references to spades and crowds.
12   Consider Wilde's use of dramatic irony in this scene.

The insults stop when Jack enters. He is followed a few minutes later by Algernon. They are forced to admit their true identity. The women turn to each other for support as they realize they have both been deceived. Left alone in the garden, the two men rebuke each other and reveal that have both arranged to be re-christened Ernest.

## WRITING ACTIVITIES

13   Produce a graph to track the women's relationship. Find key phrases to show how their friendship moves from one extreme to the other.
14   Produce a chart to show the trivial and serious references in Act 2.
15   What examples of epigram and paradox can you find in Act 2?

### ESSAY QUESTION: ACT 2

Compare and contrast the personality, attitudes, and lifestyle of Cecily and Gwendolen. Are they too superficial to be taken seriously?

ACT 3

The women ask for an explanation of the deception and are flattered by the answers, but names still present a problem, until the men reveal their intention of being christened that afternoon.

Lady Bracknell interrupts the reconciliation. On hearing of Algernon's engagement to Cecily, Lady Bracknell finds out what she can about her to assess her suitability. She is not impressed until she discovers that Cecily has investments worth £130,000 – then she gives her consent. Jack, however, refuses to allow his ward to marry Algernon on the grounds of his dishonesty. He tries to bargain with Lady Bracknell – he will give his consent for Cecily to marry Algernon if Lady Bracknell will allow Gwendolen to marry Jack.

## WRITING ACTIVITIES

**16** What is the effect of Cecily and Gwendolen speaking at the same time and the men replying in the same way?

**17** Lady Bracknell asks if Bunbury was the victim of a revolutionary outrage. Find out about attacks by anarchists in the 1890s. What do they add to your understanding of society at the time the play was written?

**18** Explain the irony behind Jack's reasons for not letting Cecily marry Algernon.

When Dr Chasuble enters, his mention of Miss Prism startles Lady Bracknell. Miss Prism enters soon after – and Lady Bracknell immediately demands to know where the baby is.

It is revealed that, 28 years previously, Miss Prism disappeared with a baby boy in a pram. When the pram was found, it contained the manuscript of a three-volume novel. Miss Prism explains that she had mistakenly put the baby in her bag and the manuscript in the pram. Jack fetches the handbag in which he was found – it turns out to be Miss Prism's bag. Further questioning reveals that Jack is Algernon's elder brother, and he was really christened Ernest. Everything is now set for a happy ending.

## WRITING ACTIVITIES

**19** Complete your chart of serious and trivial references for Act 3.

**20** What examples of epigram and paradox can you find in Act 3? Comment on how they work and the effect they produce.

**21** To what extent is the play dependent upon coincidence?

### ESSAY QUESTION: ACT 3

What factors contribute to the humour of the ending?
Consider:

- character
- language
- coincidence
- confusions and mistaken identity.

# CHARACTER

As you read through the play, you need to keep track of the individual characters and collect information about them.

We will begin by tracking **Jack**. First of all, what facts do we know?

1 He is in love with Gwendolen. How do we know? Find the evidence that proves these facts.

- He has travelled to London to propose to her.
- He calls her 'Gwendolen' rather than the formal 'Miss Fairfax', as would have been more usual.
- He undergoes a grilling by Lady Bracknell.
- He is prepared to change his name for her.

Now consider what the following tell us about his personality:

- Why is he in the position of having to change his name?
- Why does he first talk about the weather?
- Why does he not tell the truth when he had planned to?

2 He takes his responsibilities as Cecily's guardian seriously. How do we know? Find the evidence that proves these facts:

- He wants to 'kill off' his imaginary brother because of her curiosity.
- He has provided her with a governess.
- He is upset by Lady Bracknell's tone when she is asking about Cecily's suitability as a wife for Algernon.
- He does not want Cecily to marry a self-indulgent character.

3 As a baby, he was abandoned. He was apparently left in a handbag – which he still keeps – at Victoria Station. What can you deduce from the fact that he has kept the handbag?

What else can we deduce about Jack? Consider the following:

- he is deceptive
- he eats when he is nervous
- he is cunning
- he tries to protect Cecily from Algernon
- he dislikes Lady Bracknell's snobbery.
- he has two identities
- he can be romantic
- he enjoys society life

Find evidence for these points and add as many as you can.

Create a character map to show the two sides of Jack. It has been started for you on the next page.

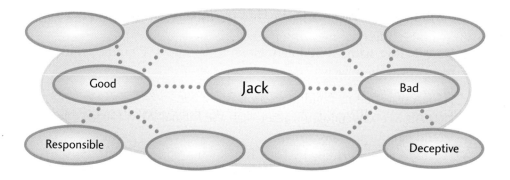

## ESSAY QUESTION: JACK

To what extent do you consider Jack Worthing to be an admirable character?

Make sure you track all of the characters as you go through play. For example, when considering **Algernon**, some key aspects are:

- he is the nephew of Lady Bracknell
- he is a member of upper-class society
- he has an imaginary friend – Bunbury – to help him escape from society when he needs to
- he is sharp – for example, he notices how much has been drunk
- he has discovered something about Jack that he will use to his own advantage
- he does not want to upset his aunt.

Less obvious points about Algernon include:

- he is a 'dandy'
- he does not take life seriously
- he enjoys breaking rules
- he is honest with himself.

Algernon utters many of the key witty sayings. Consider what you can learn about him from the following – and other – things he says:

- 'If the lower orders don't set us a good example, what on earth is the use of them?'
- 'Divorces are made in Heaven.'
- 'It is absurd to have a hard and fast rule about what one should read and what one shouldn't.'
- 'The truth is rarely pure and never simple.'
- 'The amount of women in London who flirt with their own husbands is perfectly scandalous.'

Keep track of what Algernon says and does, and create a character map like the one for Jack.

Now consider the two men in contrast to each other. In what ways are they similar? How do they differ? Do you find it easy to believe that they are brothers?

Go on to consider **Gwendolen** and **Cecily** – first Gwendolen, then Cecily, then together, looking for points of comparison and contrast.

**Lady Bracknell** is obviously important. Find evidence to support the following (you should be able to find more than one piece of evidence for most):

- she is dominant and intimidating
- she is a snob
- she strictly follows social conventions
- she is highly materialistic
- she seems to have no feeling for her husband
- she does not consider other people's feelings
- she is unscrupulous
- she will bribe people to get what she wants
- education is not important to her
- she dismisses facts and considers the expectations of fashionable society to be more important.

**Miss Prism** and **Dr Chasuble** have smaller roles but are still important. Consider their personalities, their importance to the plot, and also the section of society that they portray.

## EXAMINATION QUESTIONS

1 Compare and contrast Algernon and Jack.
2 Focusing in particular on Lady Bracknell, examine the ways in which Wilde is making fun of the upper classes in the 1890s.
3 'A serious play for trivial people' was Wilde's subtitle. To what extent do you agree with this assessment?
4 To what extent do you find Gwendolen an interesting character? In what ways is she more or less interesting than Cecily?
5 Consider the various ways in which Wilde achieves comic effects in *The Importance of Being Earnest*.
6 Examine Wilde's use of witty language and dialogue, including paradox, epigram, and puns. Are the words more important than the characters?
7 In what ways can the play be considered an exposé of the society of the 1890s?
8 To what extent do you consider lies and deception to be the play's key theme?

# AN INSPECTOR CALLS

## J. B. Priestley

> *Before beginning this unit, go back to pages 2–3 and read again what examiners are looking for in an essay about post-1914 drama.*

## BACKGROUND AND CONTEXT

*An Inspector Calls* was written in 1945, towards the end of World War Two, but set in May 1912. Priestley uses hindsight and historical facts to present a thought-provoking play that addresses the issue of social responsibility. He reveals the smugness of the wealthy industrialists, yet also tries to convey a sense of hope as members of the younger generation seem ready to learn.

Between the years 1912 and 1945, numerous major events affected Britain and the entire world:

- ◆ 1912 – the coal strike, April 14-15, mentioned by Birling
- ◆ 1912 – the sinking of the *Titanic*
- ◆ 1914 – the outbreak of World War One
- ◆ 1917 – the Russian Revolution
- ◆ 1926 – the General Strike
- ◆ 1930s – the Great Depression
- ◆ 1939 – the outbreak of the World War Two.

### RESEARCH ACTIVITY

In groups, find information about the social effects of one of these events, and prepare a presentation about your findings. Try not to get bogged down in the details of what happened – we all know that the *Titanic* sank! You need to find out why the building of the ship was such a great achievement, and assess the impact of its sinking. For all of the events, find out the social climate that led to them and the impact they had on ordinary people.

# SETTING

The play is set in the fictional northern industrial town of Brumley. All of the action takes place in the dining room of factory owner Arthur Birling. Priestley gives detailed instructions for stage design.

> **WRITING ACTIVITY**
>
> 1 Study the details of the setting and sketch the stage as you see it, either from the audience's viewpoint or from a bird's eye view.
> 2 What does the setting tell us about Birling and his family?
> 3 Unity of place is one of the 'three unities' of classical Greek drama. What are the advantages of having only one set for the whole play?

# PLOT AND STRUCTURE

The story-line is very straightforward, and there are no complicated sub-plots. The action probably lasts less than two hours – the time it takes for the play to be performed on stage. Unity of action and unity of time are the other two unities in classical Greek drama – unity of action means there is a single plot, and unity of time means that all the action takes place within a day.

Arthur Birling, a 'prosperous manufacturer', and his wife Sybil are celebrating the engagement of their daughter, Sheila, to Gerald Croft, the son of rival manufacturers Sir George and Lady Croft. Sheila's brother, Eric, is also present. The atmosphere is cheerful and relaxed.

Birling is clearly delighted at the engagement and talks about the future with a confident and smug optimism. After the ladies and Eric leave the room, he confides to Gerald that he may receive a knighthood in the next Honours List. When Eric returns, Birling explains his belief that people should look after themselves and their family, and not be concerned about other members of the community.

The evening is interrupted by the arrival of Inspector Goole, who is investigating the suicide of a young girl, Eva Smith. During the course of the play, he reveals how each member of the family, and Gerald, were involved in some way with this girl:

- Birling sacked her two years previously because she was involved in strike action.
- Sheila caused her to be sacked from her next job in a department store.

- Gerald kept her as his mistress, but ended the relationship when it suited him.
- Eric got her pregnant.
- Mrs Birling persuaded a charity to reject her plea for help.

After Gerald is questioned, he goes out for a walk, only to return after Goole has left with the news that he is probably not a real police inspector. Birling verifies this by phoning the Chief Constable. The older generation, including Gerald, are relieved that there will be no court case.

The discussion moves on to the dead girl's identity. Gerald phones the Infirmary and discovers that there is no dead girl. He, Arthur, and Sybil, are completely reassured and prepared to forget the whole thing, but Sheila and Eric have learnt a sense of responsibility.

A sudden phone call announces the imminent arrival of a police inspector, who wants to ask them some questions about a dead girl . . .

## RESEARCH ACTIVITY

Investigate the rules of the 'three unities' in classical Greek drama, and consider why they were considered important. *An Inspector Calls* is a clear example of a play following those rules. Discuss what you think Priestley hoped to achieve by this. Was he successful?

## WRITING ACTIVITY

Select one of the characters involved with Eva. Imagine he or she has been asked to write a statement for the police, and produce this statement, writing in the first person. Make sure you use details from your chosen character's responses to the Inspector's questions. In the case of Gerald, for example, you could include quotations such as 'I insisted on Daisy moving into those rooms.'

## ESSAY QUESTION: PLOT AND STRUCTURE

How has Priestley structured the play in order to sustain tension? Consider:

◆ the basic simplicity of the plot
◆ the order in which the characters are questioned
◆ the continuous action
◆ Priestley's use of entrances and exits
◆ the contrast between the opening and closing scenes.

# THEMES AND ISSUES

## GUILT AND HONESTY

The Inspector tells the family 'we'll have to share our guilt'. Sheila and Eric certainly feel guilty about their part in the tragedy – the Inspector's questioning only makes them admit to guilt they already have.

Eric 'checks himself' when he is about to share a memory about women and clothes. There must also be some explanation for his heavy drinking. Sheila becomes 'agitated' when the Inspector explains that a customer complaint led to Eva being sacked from Milwards.

At the beginning, Gerald is keeping something secret from Sheila; she is clearly not convinced that he was too busy to see her the previous summer. But does he feel guilty about this? Does he feel guilty about his involvement with the dead girl? He seems almost proud of the fact that he was 'the most important person in her life'. He says that Daisy 'didn't blame me at all', so why should he blame himself?

Once Sheila and Eric have admitted to their guilt, they are able to learn from the experience. Gerald does not learn anything. Similarly, Mr and Mrs Birling feel no guilt about the way they treated Eva. Birling 'was quite justified' and his wife can 'accept no blame for it at all.' Their conviction that they did nothing wrong prevents them from learning from the experience. Apart from Mrs Birling's lie about recognizing the photograph, she speaks honestly about what she did and what she believes, as does her husband.

## WRITING ACTIVITY

Of the five characters involved with Eva Smith, whom would you say was the most honest? You need to consider their words, actions, motives, and response to the evening's revelations, as well as aspects such as being honest to themselves and to others. Remember to include short quotations to support your opinions.

## RESPONSIBILITY AND BLAME

'You talk as if we were responsible.' The 'chain of events' revealed by the Inspector shows the involvement of all five characters, but who is most to blame for the girl's suicide? Birling is adamant that he 'can't accept any responsibility'. Mrs Birling tells the Inspector to 'go and look for the father of the child. It's his responsibility'. All five are certainly to blame to some extent, but are some more responsible than others? Although many readers are critical of Mr and Mrs Birling because they 'don't seem to have learnt anything', they genuinely believe they acted appropriately given the circumstances. Gerald, Sheila, and Eric, on the other hand, were more selfish.

### DISCUSSION ACTIVITIES

1 Consider the actions of the characters from their point of view. In pairs or small groups, take each of the five characters in turn and consider:
   ◆ exactly how they were involved with the girl
   ◆ how they treated her
   ◆ their reasons for behaving as they did
   ◆ their reaction to the Inspector's revelations.
2 Consider who had the most to learn and the most to feel guilty about. Try to put them in order, and answer the question 'Who do you blame the most?' Justify your answer.

### WRITING ACTIVITY

Which of the five characters involved with Eva Smith do you think behaved the most responsibly? Base your answer on the discussion points raised in the activities above, and justify your answer with quotations.

### ESSAY QUESTION: THEMES AND ISSUES

In his final speech, the Inspector says 'We don't live alone. We are members of one body. We are responsible for each other'. To what extent does this sum up the main theme of the play?

# CHARACTERS

Priestley gives us information about the characters when they first appear; Sheila, for example, is 'a pretty girl in her early twenties'.

We can learn more from the stage directions, which describe tones of voice and reactions. In Act One, Eric 'eagerly' joins in the conversation about women's attitudes to clothes, 'but he checks himself' and is then 'confused' – this suggests that he has a guilty secret.

We can learn even more about characters from what they actually say in response to other characters and the revelations about what has been going on. Soon after Goole's arrival, for example, Birling talks about his position as alderman and Lord Mayor, and the fact that he is still a magistrate. This shows the value he places on social standing, and his belief that he is a man whose help is needed by the Inspector. It never occurs to Birling that he might be guilty in some way.

As you read through the play, build up a set of notes on each of the characters, their attitudes, and their reactions to others and to events. Include brief quotations to back up your ideas. Like any police inspector – you need the evidence!

BIRLING

Let's consider, for example, Arthur Birling. He is described as:
* 'heavy-looking'
* 'rather portentous'
* 'in his mid fifties'
* 'rather provincial in his speech'
and he has a wife who is his 'social superior'.

From this we can deduce that he speaks with a northern, probably Yorkshire, accent, he is wealthy and he is a social climber.

## DISCUSSION ACTIVITY

How can all of this be deduced from Priestley's brief introduction? Does accent matter?

We go on to learn that Birling:
* has bought the same port as Sir George
* thinks Lady Croft may be disappointed with the engagement
* is expecting a knighthood
* plays golf with the Chief Constable
* is quick to tell the Inspector that he is still a magistrate
* tells Sheila to ask for the ring back.

## WRITING ACTIVITY

Find the quotations that prove the points in the bullet list above, all of which add to our understanding of him as a snob and a social climber.

Birling is, in his own words, 'a hard headed man of business'. He shows how success and profit mean more to him than people:

* The engagement will reduce the rivalry between Birling & Co and Crofts Ltd.
* They can work together for low costs and high prices.
* He does not accept responsibility for members of the community beyond his family.
* When his workers asked for a pay rise, he 'refused, of course'.
* He sacked Eva Smith even though she was a 'good worker'.

Birling never gives an inch on this, not to Sheila:

'The girl had been causing trouble at the works. I was quite justified.'

nor to Eric:

'If you don't come down sharply on some of these people, they'd soon be asking for the earth.'

nor to Goole:

'It's my duty to keep labour costs down.'

He reacts angrily to the Inspector's attitude and method of questioning, as he feels he, Arthur Birling, former Lord Mayor, should be treated with more respect. 'I don't like your tone nor the way you're handling this inquiry.' He is obviously not used to having his decisions questioned and is 'surprised' when the Inspector asks why he refused to give his workers a pay rise.

He is also a rather unfeeling person. Eric says he is 'not the kind of father a chap could go to when he's in trouble'. This is a comment he cannot accept: 'Don't talk to me like that.' He seems to rule at home in the same way as he rules at work, and is quick to issue orders; he instructs Sheila to 'take your mother along to the drawing room', and insists that Eric will pay all the money back. He is unable to listen to other people's opinions. For example, he says to Sheila: 'If you've nothing more sensible than that to say, Sheila, you'd better keep quiet.' After the Inspector has gone, he immediately turns on Eric: 'You're the one I blame for this.' He has no understanding of how his son is feeling. He is selfishly concerned about not being awarded a knighthood and is anxious to avoid a 'public scandal'.

When the Inspector's identity has been found to be false, Birling relaxes and makes fun of Eric and Sheila. However, he is 'panic-stricken' after the final phone call.

## WRITING ACTIVITY

Do you agree that Arthur Birling is proud, selfish, and unfeeling? Write about:
◆ the way he treated Eva Smith and his response to her death
◆ his social aspirations
◆ his treatment of Eric
◆ his attitude towards the Inspector.

## OTHER CHARACTERS

Following a similar procedure, build up character studies of the other characters. You need to consider:
◆ physical details
◆ what they say and how they say it
◆ their reaction to the evening's revelations
◆ their relationship with other characters
◆ their involvement with the dead girl.

## EXAMINATION QUESTIONS

1 What do you learn about the different attitudes of people in 1912, as revealed by the characters in the play?

2 At the end Sheila says that her parents and Gerald are 'ready to go on in the same old way'. Do you agree that only Sheila and Eric have been changed by the evening's events?

3 'We are learning something tonight,' says Mrs Birling in Act Two. What does she learn and what does it tell you about her attitudes and lifestyle? Is she wholly dislikeable?

4 The play has been described in this way: 'Goole, investigating a girl's death, calls on the Birlings. Tension builds as he dissects the hidden vices and confusions behind the façade of this outwardly virtuous Edwardian household.' How does Priestley sustain this tension?

5 'Public men, Mr Birling, have responsibilities as well as privileges.' How does Goole make us realize that we are all responsible for what happens to others?

# PYGMALION

## George Bernard Shaw

> *Before beginning this unit, go back to pages 2–3 and read again what examiners are looking for in an essay about post-1914 drama.*

## BACKGROUND AND CONTEXT

### GEORGE BERNARD SHAW

Shaw was born in Dublin, into a Protestant family, in 1856. He lived to the age of 94, dying in Hertfordshire, England in 1950. For the first part of his long and successful life, Shaw was a journalist and critic. He wrote about books, pictures, music, and plays. He was a very perceptive and clever writer with an Irish wit and important ideas. During the 1880s he became interested in socialism, then a fairly new political theory. The Fabian Society was becoming known for putting forward socialist theories and Shaw became one of their leaders. He wrote pamphlets for the Fabians and spoke about socialist ideas. Shaw was outspoken, critical, and sometimes outrageous in his views.

One socialist idea is that poor people should be able to better themselves or improve their position in society through education – as Eliza does in the play.

Shaw became a serious and well-respected writer on political and economic subjects before breaking out in a new direction as a playwright in 1892. *Pygmalion* was first published in 1916.

### RESEARCH ACTIVITIES

1   What was the Fabian Society? Why was it called that? What were its members' main beliefs?
2   Find out some more about George Bernard Shaw's personal life and 'Shavian' ideas – including some of the more outrageous ones.
3   Research the extent of Shaw's work and interests by looking up a list of his complete writing.

## THE SOCIAL AND HISTORICAL CONTEXT OF THE PLAY

The year of the play is 1914, and Queen Victoria has been dead only 13 years. The 'Edwardian Summer' is coming to an end and World War One is about to start. Britain has recently fought a bloody war in South Africa. The country has a thriving economy trading world-wide, and a position of importance in world affairs. But there are clear divisions in society. The poor are severely disadvantaged and many of the rich are idle and unconcerned about the plight of others. Education has been available for the children of the poor since 1870, but is not compulsory and is not taken up by the poorest in society. There is no system of social security for the most destitute, except the remnants of the workhouse system. Children and young people in large cities like London live by their wits, often on the streets, doing a variety of menial jobs: selling things, touting for other businesses, begging, or living on the edge of crime. Britain is a wealthy country because of its industry, trade, and Empire. Many find employment in 'service': working as servants, housemaids, cooks, and butlers. Middle-class and upper-class families often employ many servants, and these jobs are considered desirable. Factories, shops, and the new department stores are other sources of employment for the lower classes, often with long

hours and poor pay. The poor in London who are not in service live in over-crowded rooms in the maze of streets and back-alleys, with no basic facilities such as electricity or running water. For the middle and upper classes, life is very different. The opulence of a wealthy country is theirs to enjoy in their large, elegant town houses with theatres, restaurants, art, parties, and with social chit-chat to amuse them.

## THE CULTURAL CONTEXT OF THE PLAY

The cultural divide of the play is between the lifestyle and interests of the lower classes, represented by Eliza Doolittle and her father, and those of Higgins and, particularly, his mother. The cultural difference is part of Higgins's challenge. Mrs Higgins realizes, as does the audience, that the difference between a flower seller and a duchess is not just phonetic (the way they speak). Cultural pursuits are also mentioned; Covent Garden is the site of the opera house – which is where Freddy and his party have probably been – as well as a site for hawkers and flower sellers. The detail of Mrs Higgins's genteel drawing room is also culturally relevant.

## LITERARY TRADITION AND THE PLAY

In the preface, Shaw says that the play is 'intensely didactic', which means that he wants to teach the audience something. Plays which 'teach', or present a moral point of view, are part of a literary tradition going back to the morality plays of the Middle Ages.

The play is also a social commentary. It satirizes the classes it presents, and it is also humorous and to some extent a comedy of manners. All of these features are aspects of literary tradition.

### RESEARCH ACTIVITIES

4   Find out what you can about ordinary day schools in 1914 and the rules about attending.

5   Find pictures or descriptions of the houses of the rich in London at this time.

6   Research the conditions of the poor in their alleyways.

7   Make a time-line of the main historical events around 1914.

### WRITING ACTIVITIES

1   From Act I, read the description of Angel Court, where Eliza lives, and compare it to the description of Mrs Higgins's drawing room at her Chelsea Embankment home in Act III.

2   What is your early impression of Clara from Act I? List some words of your own to describe her.

3   From what level of society is Eliza? What does she tell Pickering she wants and needs to do about it in Act II? Quote and comment.

## THE PYGMALION MYTH

The Greek myth, from Ovid, tells the story of Pygmalion, a sculptor and inhabitant of Cyprus. Dissatisfied and disgusted by the women he sees about him, he creates a statue of an ideal woman of extraordinary beauty, with which he then falls excessively in love. The love goddess, Venus, pities Pygmalion in his frustration and brings the statue to life. She becomes Galatea, his flesh-and-blood bride.

### How does the myth fit the play?

Shaw adapts the myth by making Henry Higgins, an expert in phonetics, adopt the role of Pygmalion. Rather than creating a statue, he takes up the case of Eliza (at her own request initially) whose cockney accent marks her out as being at the very bottom of the English class structure. Higgins 'sculpts' her pronunciation, changing her speech, so that she can pass herself off as a duchess at a society party.

How does the play differ from the myth?

Although Eliza represents Galatea, Higgins does not 'create' her for his own emotional, sentimental, or sexual purposes. He does it for a bet. There are hints at the end of Act V of a possible spark of emotion on Higgins's part, and Shaw makes reference to Eliza's feelings in his Sequel.

### RESEARCH ACTIVITY

**8**   Find and read Ovid's *Pygmalion*.

### WRITING ACTIVITIES

**4** Read the end of Act V from, Eliza: 'I don't care how you treat me . . .' to Eliza: 'I wouldn't marry you if you asked me . . .' (pages 132-135)
  - Explain what Higgins and Eliza are saying to each other here.
  - What hints are there of any possibility of a romantic relationship?
  - What is typical or otherwise about their characters in this scene?

**5** Read the last paragraph of Shaw's Sequel to the play.
  - What is his assessment of the relationship between Higgins and Eliza at the end of the play?
  - How does he say this fits with the Pygmalion myth?

**6** Look carefully at the picture on the right. It is a poster from a National Theatre production of the play.
  - Explain what you see in the picture.
  - How does what you see fit the Pygmalion myth and the play?

## PLOT AND STRUCTURE

The table on page 26 covers Act I, and shows:
- the setting
- a summary of the plot and action in the 1916 stage version
- additional information from the 1941 printed film version
- the characters who appear in the act
- the themes relevant to the act
- the dramatic function of the act
- the dramatic significance of the act.

### WRITING ACTIVITY

The plot and structure table has been completed for Act I. Your task is to copy and complete the table for the rest of the play.

| Act I | | | | | Act II | Act III | Act IV | Act V |
|---|---|---|---|---|---|---|---|---|

### Setting
London, Covent Garden beneath the porch of St Paul's church where people are sheltering from the rain. 11.15 p.m.

### Plot
A mother and daughter, Mrs and Clara Eynsford Hill, are sheltering from the rain awaiting a cab which Freddy, the son, has failed to obtain. Clara is complaining. Freddy knocks over the basket of flowers belonging to Eliza, the flower seller. The mother pays for the spoilt flowers.

  A gentleman arrives. A bystander states that a 'bloke' is taking down everything Eliza is saying. Eliza becomes hysterical, thinking she might be arrested for doing nothing wrong. There is general confusion.

  The note-taker, Professor Higgins, and the gentleman, Colonel Pickering, introduce themselves to each other, having established their mutual interest in phonetics. Higgins is rude to Eliza but claims he could pass her off as a duchess. The rain stops, people depart. Higgins, out of some remorse, throws money at Eliza who, bidding farewell to Freddy, takes a taxi home.

### Film script
The film script develops the taxi ride home, enabling the poverty and dinginess of Angel Court, Eliza's address, and her lodging to be described.

| Act I | | | | | Act II | Act III | Act IV | Act V |
|---|---|---|---|---|---|---|---|---|

### Characters
Mrs Eynsford Hill, Clara, and Freddie
Eliza Doolittle
Professor Henry Higgins
Colonel Pickering
Bystanders
Taximan

### Themes
People's rights
Self-respect
Phonetics
Education
Success and self-improvement

### Dramatic function
Introduces setting, context, and main characters.
Establishes historical and cultural background for the modern reader.
Establishes tone and mood, e.g. humour, pathos.
Establishes some basic thematic ideas.
Engages the audience.

### Dramatic significance
Shows contrast/polemic between Eliza and Clara.
Gives a first impression of Higgins's rudeness and bullying character.
Presents a clear picture of the lowliness of Eliza's life.

## ESSAY QUESTIONS: PLOT AND STRUCTURE

1 Write an essay which explores the structure of the plot and the dramatic function of Act I. In your answer, you should remember that Act I:

  ◆ introduces setting, context, and main characters
  ◆ establishes the historical and cultural background for the modern reader
  ◆ establishes tone and mood, e.g. humour, pathos
  ◆ establishes some basic thematic ideas
  ◆ engages the audience.

2 Compare the plot development, dramatic function, and dramatic significance of the following two scenes from the play:

  ◆ the scene between Eliza, Pickering, and Higgins in Act II (pages 36-46)
  ◆ the scene in Mrs Higgins's drawing room in Act III, up to Eliza's departure (pages 68-81).

Use your plot and structure table to help you plan the essay.

### Remember:

  ✔ plan your essay following the prompts given and your table
  ✔ refer to the action, narrative development, and characters
  ✔ answer fully with a well-structured and clear script which will be useful for revision
  ✔ quote from the play briefly but often, and include page references after each quote.

# THEMES AND ISSUES IN THE PLAY

The play touches on a wide range of themes and issues, reflecting the interests, prejudices, and beliefs of its author:

  ◆ phonetics/speech/pronunciation
  ◆ society/class structure/life chances
  ◆ class consciousness/style/manners/ways of being
  ◆ education/didacticism/training/bettering oneself
  ◆ behaviour/approach to life
  ◆ treatment of others/individual worth/hierarchy
  ◆ love/sentimentality/personal relationships
  ◆ women.

Some of these themes and issues overlap.

## WRITING ACTIVITY

Six categories of themes and issues are presented in the table on the following two pages. Track references to these themes and issues throughout the play, act by act. This can be done on a second reading, or as a class/group activity.

EXAMPLE

For the third theme, 'education/didacticism/training/bettering oneself', although these issues are touched upon throughout the play, the focus will be found in the Preface, Act II, the film script at the end of Act II, and the end of Act III.

## How character and action relate to theme

### Theme: phonetics/speech/pronunciation

♦ Higgins decides to change Eliza's cockney accent and dialect, because it will keep her in the gutter. He is an 'enthusiastic hero' of phonetics (sounds of a language).
♦ Higgins's phonetic abilities create humour in Act 1.
♦ Shaw's enthusiasm for phonetics and concern at their neglect by the English is the main reason for writing the play.

### Theme: society/class structure/life chances/style/manners

♦ Eliza is at the bottom of the social class structure. She wants to better herself by speaking like a lady.
♦ Higgins is professional/academic middle class, though his cynicism and scientific enthusiasm set him aside from social class. He despises class while recognizing its effects – a position which Shaw held. Higgins's manners reflect this.
♦ The Eynsford Hills are the genteel poor (Shaw's own family was in this position). They have social status but no money. Clara, for whom fashion and display are all, does not understand this. Their manners are superficial, their chances bleak.
♦ Money is a recurrent motif in the play, particularly in Acts I and II.
♦ Pickering has genuine old-fashioned class. As an ex-India and army man, he has style and impeccable manners, which is why Eliza relates to him particularly.
♦ Mrs Higgins has middle-class social status of a genteel kind, as her furnishings indicate. She has style, manners, and compassion.
♦ Mr Doolittle has an eccentric view of class. He distinguishes between those regarded as being the 'deserving poor' (those held to be deserving of charity) and the 'undeserving poor'. He resents having 'middle-class morality' forced upon him.
♦ The simplicity of the lower classes as described by Eliza is ridiculed by Higgins, but this may be more genuine than the lifestyle of the Eynsford Hills.
♦ The paradox that money and betterment through 'education' don't bring happiness is pointed out by Mr Doolittle and alluded to by Eliza and Mrs Higgins.

### Theme: education/didacticism/training/bettering oneself

♦ Eliza's desire is for education to better herself socially. Higgins's motivation is wider – to demonstrate the importance of phonetics in the language. Shaw states this as his aim in writing the play. Eliza's education is primarily about pronunciation. The play is intentionally 'didactic', i.e. it has a point to make.
♦ Shaw notes the limitations of imitating accent without being properly taught phonetics. This is the major 'education' point of the play. The social and moral question of teaching somebody to be a lady is also raised by the play. Eliza's ability to imitate an upper-class accent while lacking 'upper-class' things to say is the source of the comedy in Act III.
♦ Mrs Higgins also shows some reservations, and concern about the ultimate advantage to Eliza of her education.
♦ The film script at the end of Act II explores Higgins's teaching methods, which leave a lot to be desired.

## How character and action relate to theme

### Theme: behaviour/treatment of others/individual worth
- Higgins is insensitive and bullying in his treatment of Eliza.
- Pickering is characterized by comparatively gentlemanly behaviour.
- Mrs Higgins shows perceptive gentility and sensitivity.
- Doolittle shows naive realism and pragmatism.
- Eliza reiterates her own self-worth and self-respect a number of times in the play by saying 'I have my feelings . . .'.
- The shameful treatment of Eliza in Act IV leads her to self-realization and determination.
- The morality of the whole scheme of Higgins and Pickering is questioned.
- The moral of the tale is: you can't play with people as if they were 'dolls' without creating unhappiness, anger, confusion.

### Theme: love/sentimentality/personal relationships
- Eliza needs to be loved: 'Every girl has the right to be loved.'
- The lack of a love story between Higgins and Eliza contrasts with the nature of Eliza's love for Freddy.
- Eliza's 'secret mischievous moments' are revealed in the Sequel.
- Higgins is incapable of romantic love.
- Higgins's true feelings for Eliza remain mysterious.
- There are both strong and weak family sentiments.
- There is sentimentality in the happy ending (Sequel).

### Theme: women
- Higgins is cynical about women.
- The relationships of mothers and sons are important.
- Bachelorhood is celebrated.
- Women are sometimes dominant – e.g. Mr Doolittle's partner, and Mrs Higgins.
- The 'romantic' aspect of Higgins's feelings for Eliza are enigmatic. Shaw, who had a 40-year celibate marriage, was also puzzling in this respect.

## ESSAY QUESTIONS: THEMES AND ISSUES

1 What points does Shaw make in *Pygmalion* about education, and what is your response to them? In your answer you should include:
   - Shaw's views on the importance of phonetics, pronunciation, and speech – the didactic intention of the play
   - Eliza's desire to improve her position by speaking like a lady
   - Higgins's enthusiasm for phonetics and his project to educate Eliza
   - Higgins's methods of teaching and his approach towards his pupil
   - the moral and practical problems of the educational project with Eliza.

2 How is the theme of social class important to the play, and what are some of the complexities of class which *Pygmalion* explores? In your answer you should include:
   - Shaw's socialism and his desire for a society of more equal opportunity
   - the plight of those like Eliza in the lowest class

- ◆ what is needed to improve a person's social position – speech, manners, being accepted
- ◆ the way different aspects of class and social position are presented:
    - ❖ Mrs Higgins's style, taste, control
    - ❖ the Eynsford Hills' genteel poverty
    - ❖ Clara's assertiveness and snobbish attitude
    - ❖ Higgins's cynicism and bad manners despite his class
    - ❖ Doolittle's eccentric and satirical humour about class
- ◆ the paradox of the relationship between class and happiness.

You might answer this question best in a number of short revision essays.

**3** *Pygmalion* is concerned with the way people view others and how they treat them; with manners and behaviour. What does the play have to say about self-worth and the way to treat people? In your answer you should include:

- ◆ Eliza's view of herself at important stages throughout the play
- ◆ the way Higgins treats Eliza and others
- ◆ Pickering's old-fashioned manners
- ◆ Mrs Higgins's perceptive understanding of people and their situations.

## CHARACTERS AND THE LANGUAGE OF THE TEXT

The function of a character map like the one below is to put a picture in your mind, not only of the characters in a text, but of their relationships.

### WRITING ACTIVITIES

**1** Copy and complete the character map. Fill it out with the following characters' names:

- ◆ Colonel Pickering
- ◆ Clara
- ◆ Mrs Pearce
- ◆ Bystanders and Parlourmaid
- ◆ Mrs Eynsford Hill
- ◆ Mr Doolittle.

Think about where best to put each name.

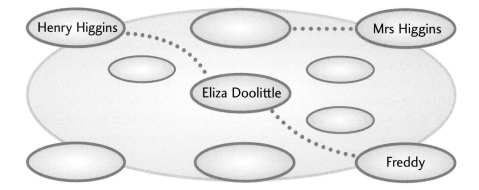

**2** Now connect the characters and write along the connecting lines the relationship between the characters, e.g. between Doolittle and Mrs Higgins write: 'Acquaintance, met once at her home'.

**NB** Leave space to add more things to this character map later.

## CHARACTER TRACKING

You will need to track characters as you read through the play, collecting key words and references for quotations as you go. Straightforward, descriptive facts are given about some of the characters. These should be collected into a table for ease of revision. An example has been started below.

| Character | Physical description | Who/what is he? Beliefs/ideas/aims | Characteristics/ relationships |
|---|---|---|---|
| Henry Higgins | He is a 'robust, vital, appetizing sort of man' – energetic, quick in movement, full of life, attractive.<br><br>He is about 40, smartly and formally dressed in 'black frock-coat with a white linen collar and black silk tie' (p 33).<br><br>He is attractive to women, e.g. Clara (p 75) and – in a complicated way – Eliza. | Higgins is a professor of phonetics, a member of the Royal Society and 'celebrated'. He is a teacher and researcher in phonetics. He is gifted in his ability to identify accent/dialect (pp 26 and 35).<br><br>He is from the professional middle class. He has a well-paid profession as an academic. He also makes money from 'educating' people out of their lower-class accents (p 26).<br><br>He believes people should not squander the 'divine' gift of speech (p 26). He has few interests outside of phonetics. He is the 'reformer–hero' of the science (Preface). | He is 'heartily, even violently interested' in his subject and all science. He is very Victorian in this respect. He is enthusiastic – to the neglect of other things (p 33).<br><br>He can be bullying, forceful, and thoughtless in what he says – but sometimes in a likeable, 'genial' way. His enthusiasm and energetic good looks help him get away with rudeness (pp 33, 74–7).<br><br>Sometimes he acts in a spoiled way, 'petulant' and short-tempered. He does not suffer fools gladly. He is rude and bullying to Eliza (e.g. Act II), to his mothers' guests (p 72 and following), to Nepommuck at the Embassy party (p 92 and following). |

# WRITING ACTIVITIES

**3** Finish the character tracking table for Higgins. Your table should sum up the analysis of the character you undertake in class. Add your impressions as they develop and change on subsequent readings and study of the play.

**4a)** Select key words from your character tracking table which will help you to revise (e.g. *energetic*, *robust*, from column 1).

**b)** Expand the character map boxes to include the key words for the characters.

You should find and learn references and quotations which support and illustrate your analysis of the character.

**5a)** In pairs or groups, select one or two exchanges from each act between Higgins and other characters, and identify what the dialogue tells you about Higgins.

**b)** Report your findings to the class with the help of an overhead projector.

**6a)** How does the language Higgins uses reflect his character – e.g. his bullying and insulting words to Eliza?

**b)** How important is the language to our understanding of the character and themes being portrayed?

## ESSAY QUESTIONS: HIGGINS

**1** Write a character analysis of Henry Higgins. Use quotations to support your points, and use your character table and the activities above to guide you.

**2** Do you think there is a change in Higgins's character after Act IV, when Eliza asserts herself and leaves him? Explain.

## EXAMINATION-TYPE QUESTION

Do you think Higgins's phonetic project with Eliza was educationally and morally justified? Explain.

# WRITING ACTIVITIES

**7** Write a character tracking table for Eliza. One has been begun for you on the next page.

**8** What do you learn of Eliza's appearance at different stages of the play? (See pages 15, 61, 77, and 88.)

**9** What do the contents of Eliza's room (pages 30-31) tell us of her ideas?

**10** Read the section in Act II from 'Pickering: Does it occur to you, Higgins, that the girl has some feelings?', to the end of the Act (pages 43-49). What do Eliza's speeches tell us of her character and state of mind?

**11** Read aloud the scene with Eliza at Mrs Higgins's 'at home'. Put on an exaggerated accent as directed (on page 77).

  ♦ What is humorous about what Eliza says?

  ♦ Why is what she says incongruous?

  ♦ What is meant by the 'new small talk'?

| Character | Physical description | Who/what is she? Beliefs/ideas/aims | | Characteristics/relationships |
|---|---|---|---|---|
| Eliza Doolittle | See activity 8 | See activities 9–13<br><br>◆ The idea of being a lady is never far from Eliza's thoughts.<br>◆ Eliza's aim is stated clearly to Pickering: 'I want to be a lady in a flower shop. . .' (p 37). | | ◆ Eliza is confident, friendly, but very soon shows vulnerability and lapses into hysterics if she thinks she's in trouble with authority figures (pp 19-20).<br>◆ She is self-pitying – she refers to herself as a 'poor girl' and feels hard done by, but enjoys the trappings of wealth, e.g. taxis (pp 28-29). |

◆ What is/was the dramatic effect of 'Not bloody likely'?

◆ How does Eliza handle the situation?

◆ What social comment is she making?

◆ How does Eliza 'give herself away' in this scene, as Mrs Higgins puts it?

◆ In what ways has Eliza been manipulated, played with like a 'live doll' as Mrs Higgins says on page 84? How has Eliza reacted to this treatment?

12 A major change happens with Eliza's character in Act IV. She says, 'I'd like to kill you, you selfish brute. Why didn't you leave me where you picked me out of – in the gutter?'(page 104). Read to the end of this scene with Higgins and carefully and analyse and evaluate what Eliza is saying. Use key words from your character tracking table.

13 In Act V Eliza says that 'the difference between a lady and a flower girl is not how she behaves but how she is treated' (page 127).

◆ What do you learn of her feelings for Pickering?

◆ Higgins seems to come close to a sentimental expression of feeling on page 133. He wants her around, but not to love – just for fun. What is Eliza's response to this?

◆ Closely analyse what Eliza and Higgins say to each other in this final scene.

◆ How does Eliza rationalize her intentions in taking Freddy as a husband (page 137)?

14 Add to the character table for Eliza, using key words (e.g. wounded, angry, proud). This will make revision easier.

## ESSAY QUESTIONS: ELIZA

1 Analyse Eliza's changing feelings and developing relationships as her character progresses throughout the play.

2 'Eliza's sense of self-worth and moral decency do not change from our first encounter with her to our last.' Do you think this is true? Explain with reference to the text.

3 Explore the development of Eliza's speech, manners, and social status throughout the play.

4 What is the emotional price Eliza has to pay, as presented in Act V, for her education and her relationship with Higgins? How does she resolve this?

## WRITING ACTIVITY

**15** Using the tables you have created for Higgins and Eliza as a model, complete a character analysis table for the characters below.

| Character | Physical description | Who/what is he or she? Beliefs/ideas/aims | Characteristics/relationships |
|---|---|---|---|
| Colonel Pickering | | He is a phoneticist with knowledge of Indian dialects. | |
| The Eynsford Hills | | | |
| Mr Doolittle | | Humorous, eccentric, a philosopher of life . . . | Prior to his change in fortune, was one of the 'undeserving poor'. |
| Mrs Higgins | | Higgins's mother, who has no illusions about her son. She has barred him from her 'at homes'. | |

## ESSAY QUESTIONS: OTHER CHARACTERS

1 In what ways is Colonel Pickering a gentleman? Why and how does Eliza respond so well to him? Comment on the language he uses (look at Act I and Act V for particular references and quotes).

2 Describe the main characteristics of Mrs Eynsford Hill and Clara. How do they contribute to the theme of 'class' in the play? (See Act I and Act III.)

3 What is Freddy like? What does Eliza think of him? Briefly describe what happens to them in the Sequel. Is this believable or sentimental? (See Act III, end of Act IV film script, end of Act V, Sequel.)

4 What does Mr Doolittle believe in? In what ways is he eccentric? What makes him a successfully humorous character? Make a close analysis of some of the language he uses (see Act II, end of Act III, Act V).

5 Describe some aspects of Mrs Higgins's lifestyle, understanding, and genteel compassion, especially towards Eliza (Act III and Act V).

### Remember:

✔ plan your essay following the components of the question

✔ make full use of your character tracking table and the activities above

✔ incorporate your key words in your answer

✔ answer fully with a well-structured and clear script which will be useful for revision

✔ quote from the play briefly but often, and include page references after each quote.

## EXAMINATION QUESTIONS

1 Shaw's belief in education as a way of helping the poorest in society is explored in *Pygmalion*. Explain how this issue is treated in the play, and what moral and personal cost it entails for the characters affected.

2 Several classes of society and their manners are explored in *Pygmalion*. Analyse Shaw's view of class, as expressed through the actions and words of his characters.

3 'You certainly are a pretty pair of babies, playing with your live doll.' This is Mrs Higgins's comment in Act III of *Pygmalion*. Analyse the treatment of Eliza by Pickering and Higgins in terms of the worth of the individual, the sensitivity of Eliza's feelings, and the morality of the entire project.

4 At the end of the Sequel, Shaw says, 'Galatea never does quite like Pygmalion: his relation to her is too godlike to be altogether agreeable.' Analyse the complexity of the relationship between Eliza and Higgins with reference to the following:

   ◆ the Pygmalion myth
   ◆ Higgins's verbal and emotional dominance
   ◆ Eliza's later assertiveness and independence
   ◆ the theme of sentimentality and love
   ◆ the play as a morality tale.

# INTRODUCTION TO POETRY

Remember that every poem is like a living time capsule. Every time you read a poem you are opening a capsule that the poet sealed when it was written. It comes alive when you read it because it comes out of the experiences, feelings, and events in the poet's life. It might come about from facing a fear in the form of a rat, as in Heaney's *An Advancement of Learning*; or the death of a mother and father as in Harrison's *Long Distance*. If you know something about the **background and context** to the writing of the poem, it certainly helps you understand how the poet's experiences might have shaped the poem.

The first thing to do with a poem is to **listen** to the words, hearing the sounds of particular groups of words. There are **rhythms** in words that are heard only when the poem is read aloud. Too often we read poems without hearing them either aloud or inside our heads.

Then **look** at the patterns on the page to see the way the lines are grouped – because poetry is not prose. The poet has structured it using a carefully chosen pattern of lines. The poet carefully chooses the *form* of the poem. It might be a 14-line poem in sonnet form, as are Claude McKay's *I Shall Return* and Shakespeare's *Shall I compare thee . . . ?*, or a free verse poem such as George Macbeth's *Bedtime Story*.

After listening to and looking at the poem you've got your first impressions, so you can ask yourself 'What's the poem about?' There's a big clue in the title. It is an important part of the overall effect, as with Tony Harrison's *Long Distance*. Is the 'Distance' a physical thing, or does it also hint at being separated in another way? Is 'Long' merely an adjective to describe distance, or does it have other associations? Thinking about this gives the reader some interesting ways into the *subject matter* and *themes* of the poem. The theme of a poem – or any other piece of writing – is what it is really about, apart from the events that happen and the people who make the events happen.

There is often an underlying meaning to the poem. For example, the themes of the separation of humans from the natural world and the power of the imagination are explored in *Roe-Deer* by Ted Hughes.

Once you've got a good idea of what the poem is about and its theme, go back over it again and read it carefully, noting the punctuation. Then pick out words that stand out for any reason. It might be because they are strange, or imaginative. They might be words that appeal to the senses, such as 'plash and gurgle' in Heaney's *Churning Day*. Looking closely at the words is getting to the heart of the poem – these are the words the poet has carefully selected to work magic with. The words are the *language* of the poem, and from comes the poem's *imagery*.

You should now have some idea of the 'voice' the poet is using in writing the poem – this is sometimes known as the poem's *tone*. It is achieved in part by the words the poet uses to set the tone (tonal words) and partly by the ideas and events in the poem. The voice the poet adopts comes in many different styles. It could be like someone telling you a secret, or someone giving you a warning. The voice could be speaking in a straightforward way or use an ironic tone. Every poem creates a mood for its reader. The reader could find a poem, such as Frost's *The Road Not Taken*, positive and hopeful. The tone may change as the poem progresses; it may begin with a light-hearted tone, but close with a more serious one, as in Charles Causley's *The Ballad of the Breadman* or Andrew Marvell's *To His Coy Mistress*.

When you have understood the poems you will have to prepare yourself for answering a question in the examination. There will be an either/or question on both pre-1914 and post-1914 poetry. In each poetry question you will be asked to compare two poems. In each case one poem will be named and you will be asked to choose another to use for comparison. Comparison means looking at any **similarities** or **differences** you find. This is sometimes known as 'compare or contrast'. The points for comparison might be:

- subject matter
- use of imagery
- voice/tone and mood
- themes
- choice of language
- form and structure.

You will not have to compare every aspect of the poems – only those you find most significant. You do not have to write equally on both poems; you can concentrate on one and use the other to highlight similarities or differences. You should spend about **40 minutes** answering the question. At the start, a reminder will be printed:

- answer the question using appropriate evidence from the texts
- explore language and structure
- look at the relationships between poems.

This section of your *Students' Book* will take you through four pairs of poems and eight individual poems. For each poem there will be help on the poem's background, subject matter, themes, tone, language and imagery, and form, followed by activities to help prepare you to write an essay. The paired poems will be compared in whatever ways are appropriate. There will also be sample questions that will be similar to the style of questions you will meet on your examination paper.

# Pre-1914 Poetry

## Keats, Rossetti, Clare, Marvell

*Before beginning this unit, go back to pages 36–37 and read again what examiners are looking for in an essay about pre-1914 poetry.*

In this unit we will first study *To Autumn* by John Keats, and *Amen* by Christina Rossetti.

## *To Autumn*: BACKGROUND AND CONTEXT

Keats was part of a literary and artistic movement known as Romanticism, which was taking place across Europe at the end of the eighteenth century. Romantics emphasized the power of the imagination and the emotions, as a reaction to the dominance of reason and intellect in the philosophy of the eighteenth century.

At the time of writing *To Autumn*, Keats was reaching both the height and the end of his writing powers. He was suffering from tuberculosis, and he died in February 1821 in Rome.

### RESEARCH ACTIVITY

Research the Romantic movement.

## SUBJECT MATTER

*To Autumn* is an ode, which is a formal address to a person or abstract idea. An ode is always serious in tone and subject matter. Here Keats addresses the season of autumn, and he balances his description of the fruitfulness of the season in the first stanza with ideas of death and decay in the final one.

### WRITING ACTIVITY

Write out one sentence each from the first and last stanza that you think sum up Keats's view of the season.

## THEMES

Keats had suffered the death of his brother Tom in 1818, and his own health was increasingly poor. The poem has clear themes of death and decay, and Keats accepts them as being part of the natural order. Ideas about youth, beauty, and truth are often found in Keats's poetry, and at the time of writing *To Autumn* ideas about the loss of youthful beauty and the transience of life were being brought home to him by illness and his passionate love for Fanny Brawne. The opening stanza, describing the time just after harvest, emphasizes the bounty of nature and the rich harvests – fulfilment of the promise of summer. The seasons are frequently used by artists as metaphors for the cycle of human life, from birth in spring to joy in summer, maturity in autumn, and death in winter.

### WRITING ACTIVITIES

1   Identify between two and four lines from the poem that best illustrate the main themes of the poem.

2   Write a comment that shows what the poet achieves in these lines.

## TONE

Look back at the introduction on pages 36-37 and remind yourself of the section that deals with the voice or tone a poet uses.

By the last stanza of *To Autumn*, the tone of the poem has changed. Look at the words in the first stanza that suggest abundance and fruition, such as 'ripeness', 'swell', and 'plump', and compare the choice of words used to indicate the change of tone in the last stanza, with 'wailful', 'mourn', and 'bleat'.

### WRITING ACTIVITY

Describe the mood or tone of the poem. Do the three stanzas have the same tone?

## LANGUAGE AND IMAGERY

The poem is full of sensual imagery. The last stanza uses mimetic effects (onomatopoeia) in the long vowel sounds to create the sounds of the buzzing gnats. In the first stanza the technique is used to create the sense of ripeness and fullness with the use of the 'o' and 'u' sounds in 'mellow fruitfulness/close bosom-friend of the maturing sun'.

The poem begins with the personification of autumn as a close friend to the sun. The opening lines use alliteration of 'm' and 's' sounds and round vowel sounds to create the impression of ripeness. In addition to the appeals to the senses of sight and sound in the first stanza, there are also appeals to the senses of smell, taste, and touch. Look how the alliteration of 'clammy cells' helps create an impression of the stickiness of honey. Words like 'core', 'gourd', and 'plump', with their full vowel sounds close together, give the impression of fullness.

In the middle stanza, autumn is personified by four human figures taken from harvest scenes. The overall effect of these descriptions of the farm workers is to emphasize their tiredness after their tasks. Listen to the onomatopoeic effect in 'oozings hours by hours.'

In the last stanza Keats refers to music, firstly of spring – with its new hopes – and then of late autumn's last days, with its more melancholy sounds. The images of death and decay and the impending winter are hinted at in 'bloom', 'soft-dying', 'mourn', 'sinking', and 'dies'.

### WRITING ACTIVITIES

1   Look again at the second stanza. Pick out the four personifications and briefly explain each worker's task. Explain how Keats uses descriptive words and images to convey the drowsiness of each figure.

2   Find at least one example of words and phrases that appeal to each of the senses. For each of these add a comment on how the effect works – such as appeal to colour, use of vowel sounds, onomatopoeia, metaphor, simile, alliteration or assonance.

## STRUCTURE AND FORM

*To Autumn* has three stanzas, each with 11 lines. The rhyme scheme is complex. The first stanza deals with autumn's attractiveness; the third makes reference to decay and the passage of time, while the middle one uses personifications to move gradually from the fullness of the first stanza towards the sense of decline in the final one. The lines are mainly end-stopped, but there are some run-on lines; for example, they are used in the first stanza to give the effect of fullness.

### DISCUSSION ACTIVITY

Why is the structure of the poem in three stanzas important for an understanding of the ideas behind the poem?

## *Amen*: BACKGROUND AND CONTEXT

Christina Rossetti was a member of the artistic Rossetti family. She had two older brothers: Dante was an artist and a writer of poetry and prose, William was an art critic and writer. In 1848 they founded the artistic movement called the Pre-Raphaelite Brotherhood, a collection of artists, poets, and critics. Although Christina was a talented writer – publishing poems under a pen name in 1850 – she was never admitted to the Brotherhood, which was a male preserve. At that time women writers were considered inferior because their work was thought too emotional, lacking the rigour and intellectual discipline of the male writers. In fact Christina Rossetti's technical skills were of a high standard and she wrote with vigour and vitality; but she did have a tendency towards melancholic themes. She had two unsuccessful romantic engagements, which may help to account for the resigned mood of some of her poetry.

## SUBJECT MATTER

The title refers to the end of a prayer to God. *Amen* means 'so be it'. If this is the case, what is the poet praying for? Each opening line of the three stanzas begins with a statement that is then turned into a question. The first stanza deals with the idea of completion of a task using the image of harvest; the second moves from ideas about autumn into images of fields left fallow as in winter; the final stanza looks beyond earthly life. Within these metaphors of the life cycle are philosophical questions about life. On first reading it appears an easy poem to understand, but on closer readings it has much more depth.

### ▌WRITING ACTIVITY

Write out the key line from each stanza that you think best summarizes the poem's subject matter.

## THEMES

*Amen* deals with philosophical questions of the meaning of existence and an individual's part in God's plan. This obviously includes big issues of life, death, the after-life, and the passage of time. The seasons are a metaphor for the cycle of life and the meaning of existence.

### ▌DISCUSSION ACTIVITY

Identify three lines from the poem that best illustrate its main themes.

## TONE

Look back at the introduction on pages 36–37 and remind yourself of the section on voice and tone.

**WRITING ACTIVITY**

Does the tone or mood of the poem change? If so where does this change take place? How would you describe the different tones?

## LANGUAGE AND IMAGERY

The language of the poem is deceptively simple. Even though it was written over a century ago there are hardly any unusual or obsolete words. But behind the deceptively simple diction lie complex ideas about life. The disappointment of what we are left with after the hard work of life is shown by the negative reply in 'Nay', the use of 'truly', the repetition of 'Now' in lines 4 and 5, and the use of 'toiled' and 'duly'. The use of 'Now' and the present tense leaves unsaid the idea of the future – what is to come after all this hard work? Rossetti seems to be asking herself or perhaps some god: each person has toiled to bring in the harvest of their life's efforts, so what is their reward? The second stanza follows a similar pattern of simple language used to ask profound questions. The ideas of unfulfilled promise and death or winter are given in the images of 'unblown' buds and 'unsown' fields. Note the neat internal rhyme at the heart of the poem in 'Lives are finished; time diminished.'

The final stanza opens with less resignation and disappointment, with the words 'reckon' and 'rightly' indicating that there is some plan at work that gives meaning to life's toils. The cycle of life is given in the last five lines, with images from nature: spring replaces the ice of winter, summer roses cover the winter thorns, and the garden becomes full of the spices of life. There are other associations at work here, with the Christian idea that there is no triumphal crown without thorns (as in Christ's passion); and the paradise of the garden of Eden teeming with life. Is Rossetti saying there may be few rewards on earth, but in heaven there is eternal happiness?

**WRITING ACTIVITY**

Choose the three most effective images from the poem and say how they work.

## STRUCTURE AND FORM

The poem has three stanzas written in iambic tetrameters. The opening line of each stanza begins with a bold statement. The key word ('over', 'finished', 'suffices') in each opening statement is then used as a question. Because of the repetition of the rhymes, especially in the final stanza, the poem resonates like a hymn or prayer. At the end of the second stanza Rossetti uses a pair of rhetorical questions. Answers to these questions are given in the longer final stanza.

### ▌WRITING ACTIVITY

Find the three single lines of description or action, and comment on their effectiveness.

## COMPARISON BETWEEN THE POEMS

Your examination answer can begin with a brief introduction to the context of the poems, but please remember this must be brief. The examiner will expect this to lead very quickly into answering the question and showing your knowledge, understanding, and appreciation of the poems' effectiveness as literary texts.

### SUBJECT MATTER

Look back at your notes on the subject matter of both poems.

### ▌WRITING ACTIVITY

1   Write a short introductory paragraph that describes the similarities and contrasts between the poems in terms of their subject matter.

### THEMES

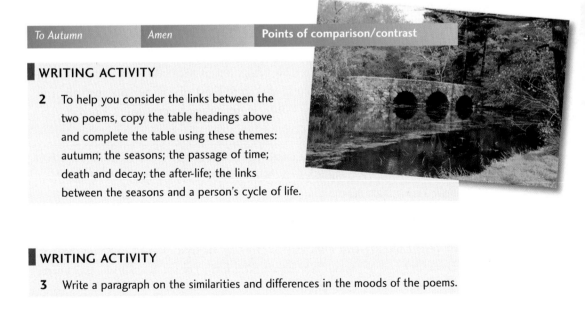

| To Autumn | Amen | Points of comparison/contrast |
| --- | --- | --- |

### ▌WRITING ACTIVITY

2   To help you consider the links between the two poems, copy the table headings above and complete the table using these themes: autumn; the seasons; the passage of time; death and decay; the after-life; the links between the seasons and a person's cycle of life.

### TONE

### ▌WRITING ACTIVITY

3   Write a paragraph on the similarities and differences in the moods of the poems.

### LANGUAGE AND IMAGERY

Many similarities in language and imagery links the two poems.

### ▌WRITING ACTIVITIES

4   Find the best examples from each poem for these language features. Some may not apply to both poems:
   ◆ language that appeals to the senses: sight, hearing, touch, smell, and taste
   ◆ examples of onomatopoeia
   ◆ examples of alliteration
   ◆ effective images, either similes or metaphors
   ◆ examples of a descriptive compound word.

5   Write two paragraphs for each poet on how they create an appeal to the reader's senses. Comment on how the effect is achieved.

## STRUCTURE AND FORM

### ▌WRITING ACTIVITY

6   Write a paragraph on the structure and form of *To Autumn* and *Amen*, showing how the division into three stanzas is used to support the ideas in both poems.

## EXAMINATION QUESTIONS

With the paragraphs you have prepared you are now ready to put together an essay to answer an English Literature examination question. The question might be like one of the following:

> **Question 1:** Look again at *To Autumn* by John Keats. Compare this poem with any other poem from the pre-1914 section of *Best Words* in which an appeal to the senses is a significant feature.
>
> **Question 2:** Compare how ideas about mortality are expressed in *Amen* by Christina Rossetti and in at least one other poem from the pre-1914 section of *Best Words*. Remember to comment on the writer's use of language.

To answer Question 1 you could use for comparison *Amen* or *First Love*, *To His Coy Mistress*, *Ballad*, *To a Mouse*, *The Flea*, *Porphyria's Lover*, or *La Belle Dame Sans Merci*.

For Question 2 on ideas about life and death you could use *To Autumn* or *First Love*, *My Last Duchess*, *To His Coy Mistress*, *Shall I compare thee?*, *Ballad*, *O Loss of Sight*, *To a Mouse*, *The Flea*, *Let me not*, *Porphyria's Lover*, or *La Belle Dame Sans Merci*.

You can see that both questions leave you with room to choose different poems. The question will not be so closed that you can answer it only with two specific poems. There will be scope for a choice of several poems for comparison. Remember that the key words of the question are the starting point for your answer. In Question 1 it is **an appeal to the senses**. In Question 2 it is **how ideas about mortality are expressed**. Keep your answer focused on the key words of the question, but you also may be able to bring in other closely connected aspects. For example, for Question 1 here you could should how aspects such as mood and theme are important in understanding how language appeals to the senses.

# First Love

Now we will consider the poem *First Love* by John Clare (1793–1864).

## BACKGROUND AND CONTEXT

Clare was of humble background and worked as a farm labourer. When his family was rehoused because of the economic changes in the countryside, the sense of loss and dislocation changed his life and led to depression and, eventually, an insane asylum.

## SUBJECT MATTER

The title makes the subject clear; Clare writes about a love that affected his whole life. His first love was Mary Joyce, and although he married another the loss of his first love caused him great sorrow. His poem describes the powerful physical effects love has upon him.

## THEME

The theme of the poem is the pain of love and the fear of rejection.

### ▌WRITING ACTIVITIES

1 Write out two lines from the poem that best illustrate the pain of being in love.
2 Add a comment that shows what the poet achieves in these lines.

## TONE

Clare writes a personal poem in which he expresses his inner feelings. There is pain, innocence, vulnerability, and anguish in his voice.

## LANGUAGE AND IMAGERY

The poem uses simple physical images to describe the emotions of being in love. The verb 'struck' in the first line gives the idea of the physical force of first love. He uses contrast for effect, such as describing how his face turns first 'deadly pale' and then 'blood burnt round my heart'. The lover's world is turned upside down and day becomes night. He describes the loss of control over his body and his emotions. There are simple yet effective images such as 'a sweet flower' and his singing heart. He hopes his loved one returns his feelings, but the evidence for this only 'seemed' to be there. The most intense pain will come if his love is not returned. To show the results of this possible rejection, images of death are included – 'my life and all seemed turned to clay' in the first stanza, and 'winter's choice' and a 'bed' of 'snow' in the last stanza. Whatever happens, his life is changed forever; the last stanza has ironic references to his family 'dwelling place' – he was forced out and could never return.

### WRITING ACTIVITY

**3**    Choose two memorable images from the poem and explain why they are effective.

## STRUCTURE AND FORM

The poem has a regular pattern of three stanzas each of eight lines with alternate rhymes. The first stanza is written in tetrameters, but the second uses alternate lines of eight and six beats, perhaps to show the struggle going on inside him. The third stanza begins with two lines of six beats each asking a question, and then follows the same pattern as the second stanza.

## COMPARISONS

*First Love* could be compared with several of the poems about love, including *My Last Duchess*, *To His Coy Mistress*, either of the Shakespeare sonnets, *Ballad*, *The Flea*, *Porphyria's Lover*, or *La Belle Dame Sans Merci*.

# To His Coy Mistress

We will now consider *To His Coy Mistress*, by Andrew Marvell (1621–1678). As with *First Love*, it could be compared with several of the poems about love.

## BACKGROUND AND CONTEXT

Marvell was a diplomat, politician, and possibly a spy. He lived at a time of political change, with the English Civil War. In addition to his poetry he wrote many prose works, and often used satire and irony for effect.

## WRITING ACTIVITIES

For each of the sections below, write a paragraph summarizing your main points. You can then use one or more of these to compare with *First Love*.

### SUBJECT MATTER

'Coy' here means 'unwilling' or 'shy' – perhaps both. The 'mistress' here means 'the woman who has his heart'. The narrator is asking his reluctant mistress to give in to his (and her) desires before her beauty is lost and time destroys both their lives.

### THEME

The main theme can be summed up in the Latin phrase 'carpe diem', which means 'seize the day' – take what you can while you can, because you do not know what the future will hold. The theme of time is summed up in the often-quoted lines: 'But at my back I always hear/Time's wingèd chariot hurrying near'.

### TONE

Marvell cleverly sustains the subtle interweaving of a witty, lightly ironic tone with profound seriousness. There are changes in tone in the poem. The first stanza uses a light, ironic tone as he describes his lady's physical attributes. In stanza 2 he uses a sombre, serious tone as he deals with death. The final stanza mixes urgency and passion.

### LANGUAGE AND IMAGERY

Look at the first stanza for the use of hyperbole for effect. His images range across time and space, from the Ganges to the biblical Flood. Marvell also describes his sexual appetite with a play upon the meaning of 'vegetable love'. Using exaggeration, he describes how her physical attributes should be adored. Memorable images such as 'iron gates of life' help make the poem Marvell's most famous.

### STRUCTURE AND FORM

The narrator's arguments give structure to the poem. The first stanza of 20 lines gives the first argument; the next 12-line stanza offers the second argument. The third stanza, beginning 'Now therefore', concludes that if the previous arguments have been accepted, the lady will give up her coyness and join with him to 'sport' their amorous 'pleasures'. The final couplet sums up the argument.

# PRE-1914 POETRY

## *Donne, Browning, 'Anon'*

> *Before beginning this unit, go back to pages 36–37 and read again what examiners are looking for in an essay about pre-1914 poetry.*

In this unit we will first study *The Flea* by John Donne and *Porphyria's Lover* by Robert Browning.

The five aspects of the poems with which we are concerned are:
- ◆ subject
- ◆ mood and tone
- ◆ analysis of imagery/language
- ◆ form and structure
- ◆ theme

The question you will be asked on poetry requires a *comparison* to be made between two or more poems. You will be expected to respond to all the aspects noted above, but the most marks will be given for presenting a *comparative analysis* of thematic meaning and language.

## SUBJECT MATTER

|  | *The Flea* | *Porphyria's Lover* | Points of comparison/contrast |
|---|---|---|---|
| Who is in the poem? | The poet, who is the lover and who is the voice of the poem, and his lady (his potential mistress). Neither have names; the mistress doesn't speak. | Porphyria, a young woman with 'smooth white shoulders' and 'yellow hair', and her unnamed, sinister lover. |  |
| How does the poet speak to the reader? | The poet is addressing the lady directly using the second person singular. This adds immediacy and some tension to the tone. |  | Donne's poem is written as the events are happening, Browning's is retrospective (looking back) until line 51. There is no speech in Browning's poem. Donne's is all speech. |
| Where and when is it set? |  | It is set in a time contemporary with the writing – mid-Victorian, inside a 'cottage', at night. The poem is a telling of the murder just after it has happened – 'And thus we sit together now'. | Both are interiors of a domestic kind, though this is not certain in Donne's case. Browning's poem takes place at and through the night. It is of longer dramatic duration than Donne's. |

| | The Flea | Porphyria's Lover | Points of comparison/contrast |
|---|---|---|---|
| What is happening? | The lover is attempting to persuade the lady to give him sexual favours. He uses logical arguments. | | Nothing dramatic happens in the Donne poem – the flea sucks their blood, then the lady succeeds in squashing it. A great deal happens in Browning's: stoking the fire, undressing, caressing, murder. |
| What are the most significant events? | | Porphyria's arrival and seductive undressing. The 'passion' of their love-making. The murder. His bizarre actions after the murder. | Clever verbal argument is contrasted with passionate deeds. There is a death in each poem. |

### WRITING ACTIVITY

Make a copy of the table above and fill in the gaps.

# FORM AND STRUCTURE

## OVERALL STRUCTURE OF *The Flea*

The form of each of the poems is interesting and very different. Donne is presenting an argument in order to persuade his lady to submit to him. He therefore writes the poem in the form of two logical arguments and a conclusion. This is a way arguments are presented in formal logic. Donne was a lawyer and was aware of the need for powerful persuasion in order to win a case.

### WRITING ACTIVITY

1 What are the main points made by the lover in his first argument in stanza 1?
2 What are the main points made by the lover in his second argument in stanza 2?
3 What are the main points made by the lover in his 'conclusion' in stanza 3?
4 What can you say about the indented last three lines of each stanza?

## METRICAL FORM OF *The Flea*

The metrical form of the poem can be described as a tetrameter (four feet) alternating with pentameter (five feet). The stress is mainly iambic (on the second syllable), with some trochaic feet (where the stress is on the first syllable) in the last stanza.

The rhyme scheme is *aabbccddd*.

## DISCUSSION ACTIVITY

As a group, discuss how you would show that the statements about metrical form and rhyme scheme above are correct. Here is a chart to help you:

| | trimeter | tetrameter | pentameter | hexameter | iambic | trochaic |
|---|---|---|---|---|---|---|
| Number of syllables | 6 | 8 | 10 | 12 | | |
| Number of feet | 3 | 4 | 5 | 6 | | |
| Stress on syllables | | | | | Unstressed first/ stressed second | Stressed first/ unstressed second |

## OVERALL STRUCTURE OF *Porphyria's Lover*

The poem is a *dramatic monologue*. In a dramatic monologue, a single fictional or historical character speaks to a silent audience, revealing his or her personality, morality, thoughts, and feelings.

The indentation and the rhyme scheme have the effect of dividing the poem into five-line sections of verse, though they are not presented as separate stanzas.

## WRITING ACTIVITY

**5** Describe exactly how the indentations work, and explain the rhyme scheme. Why might the poet not have wanted stanzas?

## METRICAL FORM OF *Porphyria's Lover*

## DISCUSSION ACTIVITY

In pairs, following the procedure you used for *The Flea*, describe and explain the metrical form of the poem.

# MOOD OR TONE

The tone of a poem is the mood it conveys or the mood it evokes in the reader. Put another way, the mood of a poem is established by the tone of the words and ideas used. Here are some random adjectives which might be applied to poems:

| | | | | | |
|---|---|---|---|---|---|
| bleak | ironic | solemn | satirical | sentimental | light-hearted |
| serious | humorous | flippant | patronizing | dismissive | detached |
| sinister | evil | warm | exciting | threatening | fearsome |
| cold | erotic | horrific | | | |

Note that the tone or mood of a poem may change as it progresses.

> ■ **WRITING ACTIVITY**
>
> Choose some of the words above which you think apply to each of the poems.
> Then think of some more of your own.
> Apply the words to different parts of *Porphyria's Lover* and notice the difference in
> the tone of different episodes in the poem.

# THEMES

The 'theme' of a poem – or any other piece of writing – is what it is really about, apart from the events which happen and the people who make the events happen.

There is usually a point being made, an underlying meaning to the poem, other than the narrative or story on the surface.

Here are some key words for each of the poems which relate to their themes. Notice, particularly, the ones they might be said to share:

| The Flea | Porphyria's Lover | Both poems |
|----------|-------------------|------------|
| psychology | obsession | seduction |
| religion | consummation | lust and love |
| persuasion | passion | murder |
|  | God | male dominance |
|  | power | jealousy |
|  |  | feminine assertion |

The table above suggests that there are six themes which are shared between the two poems, a further three about which there is something to say on *The Flea* and a further five on *Porphyria's Lover*.

Note that the themes which are not shared can be seen as 'contrasts' between the poems. Here are some notes on some of the themes.

## SEDUCTION

*The Flea* is clearly a seduction poem. The poet/lover is trying to persuade his lady to give in to his sexual desires. Here the man is the would-be seducer and it is the woman who is to be persuaded. In *Porphyria's Lover* there is also seduction. Porphyria behaves in a seductive way, between lines 6 and 25, towards her lover.

**WRITING ACTIVITY**

1 Read lines 6–25 of Browning's poem. List and quote the seductive things
Porphyria does – and the effect they have.

## OBSESSION, JEALOUSY, PASSION

Porphyria's lover is obsessed. His obsession is both mental and physical
with, for example, five mentions of Porphyria's hair. His obsession
with possessing her leads to murder and his gruesome caressing of her
dead body through the night. His jealousy of Porphyria's 'pride, and
vainer ties', and presumably other lovers, is a further aspect of his
obsession. Their passion and the feeling that 'that moment she was
mine, mine', build towards the climax of her death and the silence
after the murder.

Donne, by contrast, is calmly logical and not obsessed – though his
lady is determined and single-minded. His jealousy of the flea, which
has enjoyed more pampering and swelling than he has, is witty and
amusing. The lady holds his passion in check.

**WRITING ACTIVITY**

2 Look up the word 'Porphyria'. What do you learn which might help you in an
analysis of the poem?
3 Read carefully from line 20 to the end of the poem, noting appropriate
quotations which relate to obsession, jealousy, and passion. Contrast these
themes with John Donne's more detached poem.

## MALE DOMINANCE AND FEMININE ASSERTION

At certain points in each poem, the women assert themselves –
Porphyria does so by stoking up the fire, undressing, actively caressing
and seducing her lover. Donne's lady does so by not
accepting his arguments, and finally killing the flea.

**WRITING ACTIVITIES**

4 Track exactly the way the women assert themselves and
give quotations to support your findings.
5 When and how do the men dominate in the poems?
Explain and comment.
6 Pick out some interesting similarities as well as contrasts
in the themes of The Flea and Porphyria's Lover, using
appropriate quotations.

# LANGUAGE AND IMAGERY

A 'conceit' is an elaborate or unusual image or fact, used for effect.

> **WRITING ACTIVITY**
>
> 1 How is the flea in Donne's poem used metaphorically? What is the effect of this conceit on the reader?

In the first stanza of *The Flea*, Donne uses a number of words which have sexual connotations, and in the second he uses words and images which remind us of religion. One of these images is

> 'we're met
> and cloistered in these living walls of jet.'

This is an example of what is known as 'strong-lined verse', because the line is densely packed with imagery and meaning.

> **WRITING ACTIVITIES**
>
> 2 Find and list the words in the first stanza which you think have sexual or sensual connotations. Why do you think Donne has used these? Remember he is speaking them to the lady he is trying to seduce.
> 3 In the second stanza, how does Donne connect religious imagery with his seduction? Why does he do this?
> 4 Explain the 'strong-lined' verse quoted above.

The *pathetic fallacy* is the language device used by some poets where natural things (such as the weather) are presented in a way which is sympathetic to the mood or subject matter of the poem.

> **WRITING ACTIVITY**
>
> 5 Read the first four lines of Browning's poem and explain how this form of imagery works.

A number of vivid phrases and images are conjured up by Browning which evoke a sensual or sexual mood between lines 10 and 35. The adjectives and verbs are particularly effective.

> **WRITING ACTIVITY**
>
> 6 Find and quote vivid words and phrases which establish Browning's desired tone or mood in the poem before Porphyria dies.

As with Donne's 'strong-lined' verse, there is a density of meaning in the words used by Browning between lines 51 and 55.

# My Last Duchess

Robert Browning's poem *My Last Duchess* is based on historical fact. The wife of Alfonso II, Duke of Ferrara in Italy, died in 1561 after only three years of marriage. The rest of the detail of the poem is fictional.

SUBJECT MATTER

The poem can be analysed in sections:

| | |
|---|---|
| Lines 1–13 | The portrait is shown to a visitor. The Duke says that nobody ever looks at 'that pictured countenance' without remarking on the 'depth and passion of that earnest glance'. |
| Lines 13–31 | The Duke explains that it was not just his presence which gave his late wife pleasure (lines 13–15). She delighted in many ordinary things in life. |
| Lines 31–46 | The Duke complains that the Duchess valued lowly things and people as much as she valued him. He was unable to 'lesson' her – and anyway, to do so would have been beneath his dignity. It 'would be some stooping, and I choose/Never to stoop'. |
| Lines 46–56 | The Duke announces quite casually and coldly that these characteristics of the Duchess continued – and so he 'gave commands' and her smiles ceased altogether. We don't know whether she died from a broken heart, committed suicide, or was murdered. He then casually suggests that the two of them join the company downstairs, revealing that the visitor he is speaking to is an emissary from the Count, to whose daughter the Duke is to be betrothed. On the way he points out another of his pieces of art, a bronze of Neptune taming a sea-horse. |

**WRITING ACTIVITY**

1  Which do you think is the most powerful or moving of the sections of the poem? Quote and explain.

| Character | Attributes/key words | Line references |
|---|---|---|
| The Duke | Pompous, cynical, cold, controlling, dignified, egotistical, old, proud of his history, powerful | |
| The Duchess | Young, beautiful, free, sensitive, loving towards people and nature, naïve, innocent, joyful | |

## WRITING ACTIVITIES

2 Copy and complete the table above with references from the text. You need to discuss the key words – you may not agree with some of them.

3 What impression do you have of the late Duchess and of the Duke? Collect key words and line references.

## FORM AND STRUCTURE

The poem is a dramatic monologue, like *Porphyria's Lover*. It is written in *heroic couplets*.

Heroic couplets are rhyming couplets – *aabbccdd* – written in iambic pentameter.

## WRITING ACTIVITIES

4 Write an explanation for a group of students which shows the poem is written in heroic couplets.

5 In what ways do you think the poem is 'dramatic'? Is it 'dramatic' in the same sense as *Porphyria's Lover*?

## MOOD OR TONE

The Duke is speaking throughout the poem, so you need to decide how best to describe and appreciate the tone of his voice or the mood of the words which convey his attitude to his 'last' duchess.

## WRITING ACTIVITY

6 Is the Duke concerned, remorseful, sentimental, cold, detached, cynical, bitter . . . ?

As happened to Porphyria, the Duchess dies, and the manner of the death is central to our understanding of the poem.

## WRITING ACTIVITY

7 Write down the lines from each of the poems which are concerned with death. How are they similar or different in the tone of their delivery and action?

## THEMES

The table on the next page will allow you to cross-reference themes from the three poems in this unit so far. Look back at the previous section on 'Themes' (page 51) and compare.

| Themes in *My Last Duchess* | Notes |
|---|---|
| Jealousy | 'Sir, 'twas not/Her husband's presence only, called that spot/Of joy into the Duchess' cheek' (ll 13–15). This clearly indicates that her other innocent interests and enthusiasms annoyed him and caused him to be jealous. |
| Authority | *Find instances of The Duke's authority and control. What is the significance of Neptune and the sea-horse, ll 54–5?* |
| Dignity | The Duke speaks of 'a nine-hundred-years-old name' – his heritage and history. He also indicates that 'to make . . . clear to such an one' that this or that 'disgusts me' would be beneath his dignity (ll 33–43). |
| Intolerance | *Of what was the Duke intolerant? How did he show this?* |
| Love of life | *Quote some of the things the Duchess loved and enjoyed.* |

## ▌WRITING ACTIVITIES

**8** Answer the questions in the table above.

**9** Decide which of the themes suggested for *My Last Duchess* apply to *The Flea* and/or *Porphyria's Lover*. Add further themes which apply to all the poems.

## LANGUAGE AND IMAGERY

The Duke paints a picture for us of the Duchess and her life – more detailed than the painting he is showing to the Count's emissary.

Here are some quotations:
'The depth and passion of that earnest glance'

'that spot
Of joy [in] the Duchess' cheek'

'the faint
Half-flush that dies along her throat'

## ▌WRITING ACTIVITY

**10** Find more quotations which build our picture of the Duchess and comment on the images, colours, and textures which are suggested by the words.

**ESSAY QUESTIONS: 'MY LAST DUCHESS' AND 'PORPHYRIA'S LOVER'**

1 How does the language used by Browning in *Porphyria's Lover* differ in its effect from that used in *My Last Duchess*?

2 Analyse and discuss Browning's treatment of a number of themes common to *My Last Duchess* and *Porphyria's Lover*. In what ways does the tone of each poem complement its themes?

# Ballad: 'A FAITHLESS SHEPHERD COURTED ME'

## SUBJECT MATTER

The poem beginning 'A faithless shepherd courted me' is a ballad, which is 'traditional' – meaning that it has no known, specific author. It tells the well-worn tale of an innocent girl being deceived and betrayed by a faithless lover.

The poem can be analysed in sections:

| | |
|---|---|
| Stanzas 1–3 | These verses show the situation of the abandoned girl, and what happened to her. |
| Stanzas 4 and 5 | The key word here is 'wish'. The girl thinks of what might have been if she were 'a maid again'. The fifth stanza becomes a refrain which is repeated at the end. |
| Stanzas 6 and 7 | These verses develop the girl's memories of the relationship and the lover. |
| Stanzas 8–10 | The girl looks towards the gloom which is the only future for herself and her child. |
| Stanza 11 | This repeats the refrain of stanza 5 in which suicide is the theme, but this time it addresses the child directly. |

**WRITING ACTIVITY**

1 Which of the sections or stanzas do you think are most poignant, powerful, or sad? Explain why.

## FORM AND STRUCTURE

The poem is a *ballad*. A ballad is traditionally passed on by being spoken or sung, and is in the form of quatrains. Often it has no identifiable author. It can be adapted for particular circumstances. There is often a refrain or repeated stanza. The ballad has a simplicity of structure and rhyme which enables it to be easily learned.

## DISCUSSION ACTIVITY

Discuss how and why the form of the poem is suited to its subject matter.

MOOD OR TONE

The poem is pastoral and uses the seasons and elements of the countryside to reinforce the tone and mood.

The lover pursued her through the winter, loved her in the summer which 'brought no fears to fright', but abandoned her the next winter, which 'did darkly prove'. Cold and warm, light and dark are the tones used variously through the first part of the poem.

A covering of 'green grass', a 'pillow on a thorn', and a 'bed of clay', are images that reflect the mood of despair felt by the girl.

## WRITING ACTIVITY

2  Read the poem noting the tonal effects, and collect more tonal words and images. List five or six words which sum up the mood of the girl as she relates her tale.

THEMES

The table below will allow you to cross-reference themes from the four poems in this unit. Look back at the previous sections on 'Themes' (pages 51 and 55) and compare.

| Themes in *Ballad* | Notes |
| --- | --- |
| Honour and dishonour | The girl has lost her liberty and honour, and longs for death. |
| Suicide | *Find and note references to suicide in the poem.* |
| Rejection/betrayal | The love she offered was rejected. Her innocence and naïvety betrayed her. |
| Shame/humiliation | *How heavily does the girl feel shame? Who does she blame?* |
| Self-respect/dignity | She has lost self-respect and dignity and she feels that her child is forever doomed in the same way. |
| Male dominance | *Look at the words used throughout the poem which indicate the dominant nature of the shepherd.* |
| Religion | The girl speaks of 'My soul' and 'Our souls' being with God. |

## ▌WRITING ACTIVITIES

**3** Answer the questions in the table above.

**4** Decide which of the themes suggested for the *Ballad* apply to the other poems studied in this unit. Add further themes which apply to all the poems.

**5** Analyse and discuss, with close reference to the text, one or two of the themes presented in the poem.

**6** How does the tone of the poem reflect the seriousness of its themes?

## LANGUAGE AND IMAGERY

The poem contains both metaphors and similes. Here are four:
- the image of 'stealing' in the first stanza
- the image of the babe's pillow being 'on a thorn' in stanza 5
- the imagery related to 'beds' in stanza 6
- images related to death.

## ▌WRITING ACTIVITY

**7** Look carefully at and explain the power of the images listed above.

# EXAMINATION QUESTIONS

With the paragraphs you have prepared in the activities above, you are now ready to put together an essay to answer an English Literature examination question. The question might be like one of the following:

> **Question 1:** Why do you think *My Last Duchess* by Robert Browning is such an effective poem? You should consider:
> - how the Duke's character is revealed
> - Browning's use of words and images
>
> and compare it to one other poem with similar themes.
>
> **Question 2:** Read again *Porphyria's Lover* by Robert Browning. In this poem, the poet shows how powerful an emotion love can be. Compare this poem with another from the selection which shows love, either in a very different or in a similar light. You should refer closely to the language used in each poem.

For the theme of love, you could use *First Love*, *To His Coy Mistress*, *Shall I Compare Thee . . . ?*, *Let Me Not*, or *La Belle Dame Sans Merci*.

You can see that both questions leave you the option to choose different poems. The question will not be a closed one that you can only answer with two specific poems. There will be scope for a choice of several poems in your comparison. Remember that the **key words** of the question are the starting point for your answer.

# POST-1914 POETRY
## *Heaney, Hughes, Plath*

> *Before beginning this unit, go back to pages 36–37 and read again what examiners are looking for in an essay about post-1914 poetry.*

In this unit we will first study two poems by Seamus Heaney, beginning with *Churning Day*, followed by *An Advancement of Learning*.

## *Churning Day*: BACKGROUND AND CONTEXT

*Churning Day* is one of Heaney's early poems, written in the 1960s. It comes from Heaney's first collection, *Death of a Naturalist*. These poems capture the rural background to his life on the family farm in County Derry. Northern Ireland in the early 1960s was a traditional society, but the social and religious divisions that tore the country apart in 1969, and are still present today, were strong, dark undercurrents below the surface.

### RESEARCH ACTIVITY

Research the background to the troubles in Northern Ireland and/or Heaney's life in the 1960s/1970s.

For the troubles, try: http://www.britains-smallwars.com/ni/index.html

For Heaney, try: http://ibiblio.org/dykki/poetry/heaney/

## SUBJECT MATTER

The poem describes the churning of milk into butter by hand.

## THEMES

This poem looks back at a happy memory of his childhood and rural life. One of the main themes of the poem is the process of purification and transformation. Purification means cleaning. Transformation means changing. Obviously the cleaning and changing are part of the process of turning milk into butter. However, both themes sometimes have religious associations.

Another of the themes is the reward that comes from physical effort. The poem is full of descriptions of the hard work that goes into the making of butter by hand. From this hard physical work comes the reward, not only butter, but the satisfaction of achievement.

**WRITING ACTIVITIES**

1   Identify between two and four lines from the poem that best illustrate the main themes of the poem.

2   Write a comment that shows what the poet achieves in these lines.

# TONE

Look back at the introduction on pages 36–37 and remind yourself of the section that deals with the voice or tone a poet uses.

**WRITING ACTIVITY**

1   Which words best describe the tone of the poem?

# LANGUAGE AND IMAGERY

The most striking feature of the poem is Heaney's use of descriptive words that appeal to the senses.

The energy of this physical process can be found in the opening lines of the poem. The first line has three compound words: 'thick-crust', 'course-grained', 'rough-cast'. These words, along with 'crocks' in line 2, use alliteration with the 'k' sound to give the impression of the crustiness on top of the standing milk. The simile 'as limestone rough-cast' compares the crust on top of the milk to the roughness of the coarse cement used to cover walls. There is also the metaphor of the 'pottery bombs' for the milk containers, whose large size contrasts with the smallness of the pantry.

Look at the contrast between the vowel sounds in lines 4 and 5. Line 5 uses longer vowel sounds in 'cool porous', in contrast to the short vowel sounds of 'cud' and 'udder' in line 4.

Heaney uses the word 'plumping' to describe the sound of the boiling kettles used to clean the churn. This is an example of onomatopoeia. The description of sounds is continued with the 'busy scrubber' that 'echoed daintily on the seasoned wood' of the churn in the kitchen.

As the second stanza (or verse paragraph) develops, Heaney uses many verbs. 'Spilled', 'plunged', 'fitted', 'slugged', 'thumped', 'ached', 'blistered', and 'spattered' all build up the sense of busy activity. Some of these verbs use their short vowel sounds to imitate the action they describe, as in 'slugged' and 'thumped'. The physical energy of this busy activity is summed up in two short sentences with the same structure, a noun and a strong verb: 'Arms ached. Hands blistered.'

## STRUCTURE AND FORM

The poem is in four verse paragraphs (or stanzas) of roughly equal
length. The lines have no regular pattern of either rhyme or line
length, although most lines use the iambic rhythm of ten beats. The
poem uses a mixture of long sentences running over several lines
(enjambment), and end-stopped lines. In the middle of the poem the
line is broken, perhaps indicating the change that occurs in the
churning process.

## *An Advancement of Learning*: SUBJECT MATTER

The title of the poem refers to a phase in the poet's emotional
development – part of his growing up. It describes a step forward in
his learning about himself and the world in which he lives.
While walking on the river embankment he meets two rats.
He recalls his earlier childhood fears and remembers his
panic at their appearance in the farmyard and, more scarily,
the sounds of the rats scratching about in the loft above his
bedroom. On this occasion he stands his ground, stares out
the rats and successfully crosses the bridge over the river.

## THEMES

Again this poem remembers childhood, but here the memory is a less
happy one as he recalls both the sickening meeting with the rats and
his earlier panic when he heard them scratching 'on ceiling boards
above my bed'. A recurring feature in much of Heaney's early poetry is
a seemingly ordinary, everyday event that has a lasting effect. Here,

this is explored through the themes of maturity, facing one's fears, and an awareness of the dark threats and dangers in our lives.

The poem ends with the boy experiencing a mixture of success and loss. He stares down the rat, but then he opts for a safer route across the bridge, the one he had always deferred. He has faced down one fear, but as the rat has only 'retreated' up the sewage pipe there is always the worry that another (fear) will come to take its place.

## ▌WRITING ACTIVITY

Identify three or four lines from the poem that best illustrate its main themes. Write a comment on what the poet achieves in these lines.

# TONE

Again Heaney is using the first person, 'I', to tell the reader of the childhood memories in *An Advancement of Learning*.

## ▌WRITING ACTIVITY

Write about the kind of voice and the tone used in the poem, giving quotations to support your points.

# LANGUAGE AND IMAGERY

The poem begins with what seems a peaceful description of a walk alongside a river. A closer reading picks out the odd choice of 'nosed' as the verb to describe the movement of the river, and two adjectives 'pliable' and 'oil-skinned'. The use of 'nosed' not only prefigures the description of the rats, but also gives a weight to the movement of the river. The dirtiness of the river, with its oily pollution, is reinforced with the description of the swans as 'dirty-keeled'. Notice again Heaney's fondness for compound words.

In the third stanza, the repulsion he feels on first sensing and then seeing the rat is conveyed in the mix of alliterative sounds. The 's' sounds in 'Something slobbered', 'Smudging the silence', 'Slimed' and 'sickened so' are contrasted with the harsh 'k' sounds in 'curtly, close' and 'quickly'. 'Slobbered' and 'slimed' are also two very effective onomatopoeic words that mimic the movement and appearance of the rat. The boy feels sick and, in a 'cold sweat', turns away. After the shock of seeing another rat, the words used to describe the rat change in tone. Heaney uses 'nimbling', 'tracing', 'thrilled', 'clockworked', 'glistening', 'tapered tail', and 'raindrop eye' to describe the rats' appearance and movement, a much less horrified reaction.

## DISCUSSION ACTIVITY

Give a reason for this change in Heaney's descriptive words.

There is still some fear and disgust, shown by his choice of 'back bunched', 'insidiously listening', 'knobbed skull' and 'old snout', words which convey the physical presence of the rat. There is tension between conflicting emotions – curiosity, fear, and disgust, and his determination to overcome this fear. This tension is found in Heaney's choice of words in describing both the rat and the boy's feelings.

The boy's victory is described in the simplest of words 'I stared a minute after him.' The boy then carries on his journey but takes the bridge over the river. The taking of the bridge rather than deferring it as in the past indicate both maturity in facing fears (the 'advancement' of the title) and recognition of the fears the future might hold.

## WRITING ACTIVITY

Work through from line 9 to the end. Find words that describe the rats. Put these into two lists according to the feelings they arouse: 'Strong aversion' and 'Others'.

# STRUCTURE AND FORM

The poem is in nine stanzas of four lines. The lines have no regular pattern of either rhyme or line length, although most lines use the traditional iambic rhythm with ten beats. The poem uses a mixture of run-on and end-stopped lines.

The boy's reaction and the way he overcomes his initial panic is shown by simple, one-sentence lines of description or action, as in lines 27, 35, and 36. The memory of the panic of his younger life is again illustrated by a rush into four run-on lines for one sentence, in stanza 8.

## WRITING ACTIVITY

Find three one-sentence lines of description or action, and comment on their effectiveness.

# COMPARISON BETWEEN THE POEMS

Your examination answer can begin with a brief introduction to the context of the poems, but please remember this must be brief. The examiner will expect this to lead very quickly into an answer to the question showing your knowledge, understanding, and appreciation of the poems' effectiveness.

## SUBJECT MATTER

Look back at your notes on the subject matter of each poem.

> ### WRITING ACTIVITY
>
> **1** Write a short introductory paragraph that describes the similarities and contrasts between the poems' subject matter.

## THEMES

> ### WRITING ACTIVITY
>
> **2** To help you consider the links between the two poems, list the themes that they share.

## TONE

> ### WRITING ACTIVITIES
>
> **3** Look at the words you used to describe the tone of *Churning Day*. Are there any that could apply to both poems?
> **4** Can you add any words to describe the tone of voice in both poems?
> **5** Write a paragraph on the 'voice' that Heaney uses in describing his childhood memories.

## LANGUAGE AND IMAGERY

Many similarities in language and imagery link the two poems.

> ### WRITING ACTIVITIES
>
> **6** Find the best examples from each poem of the language features listed below. Some may not apply to both poems:
> - language that appeals to each of the senses: sight, hearing, touch, smell, and taste
> - examples of onomatopoeia and alliteration
> - effective images, either similes or metaphors
> - new verbs made from nouns or adjectives
> - examples of a descriptive compound word.
> **7** Write three paragraphs on how, in both poems, Heaney creates an appeal to the reader's senses. Comment in detail on how the effect is achieved.

## STRUCTURE AND FORM

Both poems use a mixture of run-on lines and end-stopped lines. Neither poems has regular line lengths or a rhyming pattern, but both generally conform to a regular iambic rhythm.

## EXAMINATION QUESTIONS

With the paragraphs you prepared in activities 1–7 above, you are now ready to put together an essay to answer an English Literature examination question. The question might be like one of the following:

> **Question 1:** Look again at *An Advancement of Learning* by Seamus Heaney. Compare this poem with any other poem from the post-1914 section of *Best Words* in which language is used effectively to appeal to the senses.
>
> **Question 2:** Compare the way the theme of memories and childhood is explored in *Churning Day* by Seamus Heaney and in at least one other poem from the post-1914 section of *Best Words*. Remember to comment on the writer's use of language.

For each question, you could choose the other Heaney poem for your answer, or you could use for Question 1 *I Shall Return*, *Blackberrying*, *War Photographer*, *My Grandmother*, or *Roe-Deer*.

For Question 2 on memories and childhood, you could use *Long Distance*, *The Sick Equation*, *I Shall Return*, *Once Upon A Time*, *My Grandmother*, *Afternoons*, or *The Road Not Taken*.

You can see that both questions leave you the option to choose different poems. The question will not be a closed one that you can only answer with two particular poems. There will be scope for a choice of several poems in your comparison.

Remember that the key words of the question are the starting point for your answer. In Question 1, these are: **language is used effectively to appeal to the senses**. In Question 2, they are: **the way the theme of memories and childhood is explored**. Keep your answer focused on the key words of the question, but you may also be able to bring in other closely connected aspects. For example, for Question 1 here you could show how aspects such as mood and theme are important in understanding how language appeals to the senses.

# Roe-Deer

Now we will consider the poem *Roe-Deer* by Ted Hughes.

## BACKGROUND AND CONTEXT

Ted Hughes was considered by many to be the most challenging English poet of the twentieth century. He had a difficult and creative relationship with Sylvia Plath, and for decades after her death he suffered criticism because he was alleged to have mistreated her.

Hughes always had an awareness of the power of nature, and some critics found his early works to be too violent. He wrote of the power of animals and the elemental forces of nature. He felt that modern humans had lost their intuitive connections with the natural world. *Roe-Deer* is taken from *Moortown Diaries*, published in 1989.

## SUBJECT MATTER AND THEMES

The themes of the poem are people's increasing separation from the natural world and the power of the imagination – especially the poetic imagination – to re-establish that forgotten linkage. The poem is full of symbols of this separation. In the early morning the narrator is driving in the snow along a country road. Two young roe deer appear before him in the road. As he approaches them they stare at him momentarily and then bound through a hedge and off into the fields. The man in his modern mode of transport, protected from the outside world, is driving on the man-made road through the natural world of snow, fields, and trees. The roe deer represent the natural world with which humans have lost connection. The imagination of the poet allows some connection to be re-established for a moment before the curtain of separation falls back between them. The windscreen, like a mirror, glass or reflected water, represents a dividing line between reality and imagination.

### WRITING ACTIVITIES

1   Identify between two and four lines from the poem that best illustrate its main themes.
2   Write a comment that shows what the poet achieves in these lines.

## TONE

Look back at the introduction on pages 36–37 and remind yourself of the section on voice or tone. Look again at *Roe-Deer* and decide what voice Hughes is using to tell the reader of his childhood memories. He is writing in the first person, using 'I'.

## WRITING ACTIVITIES

**3**   Which words would you use to describe the tone of the poem?

## LANGUAGE AND IMAGERY

The poem works on two levels: the descriptive detail, and the metaphorical meaning. Look at how Hughes condenses his images with compound words such as 'dawn-dirty'. There are several words that indicate the metaphor of two worlds and the separation between them: 'dimension', 'secret', 'vision', 'abnormal', 'password', 'sign', 'curtain'. There is a clear description of how the two realities come together for a moment 'where the trees were no longer trees, nor the road a road' (line 12). The evidence of the encounter and epiphany the driver experiences is quickly erased by the snow. Look at the words used in the last two lines: 'revising', 'inspiration', and 'ordinary'. These words have significance beyond their surface meaning.

## WRITING ACTIVITIES

**4**   Find examples of compound words and comment on the effectiveness of each.

**5**   Write a paragraph commenting on the significance of the words chosen to convey the representations of the two worlds.

## STRUCTURE AND FORM

The poem is written in ten pairs of lines. There is no pattern of length or rhyme. Both run-on and end-stopped lines are used. The run-on sometimes goes beyond the pair of lines. The rhythm creates the impression that the writer is addressing the reader in a direct, conversational manner.

## WRITING ACTIVITIES

**6**   Write a paragraph briefly describing the form of the poem and commenting on the effectiveness of run-on lines 5–8 and 14–18.

## COMPARISONS

*Roe-Deer* could be used for comparison with several poems from the selection. The idea of the power of the imagination could be used for all poems, but more closely with any of: *I Shall Return*, *Blackberrying*, *Churning Day*, *War Photographer*, *A Martian Sends a Postcard Home*, *Bedtime Story*, *Mirror*, or *Ballad of the Breadman*.

With the examination question below, you could take *Mirror* by Sylvia Plath as the poem for comparison:

**How does the poet stretch the imagination of the reader in *Roe-Deer* and one other poem from the selection?**

# Mirror

We will now consider this poem by Sylvia Plath. *Mirror* has natural links with *Roe-Deer* as the two poets were married when they were young, energetic, and vivacious poets.

## BACKGROUND AND CONTEXT

Sylvia Plath was an American poet, considered by some critics as the best woman poet of the twentieth century. She came from a smart Boston, New England background, and her match with Ted Hughes (a working-class Yorkshireman) seemed to be a marriage of opposites. She had suffered mental problems and took the loss of her father badly. She wrote of her troubled life and attempts at suicide at 19 in a fictionalized autobiography, *The Bell Jar*. She became more and more depressed after her separation from Hughes and took her own life in February 1963. *Mirror* was written sixteen months before.

> ### WRITING ACTIVITY
>
> For each of the sections below, write a paragraph summarizing your main points. You can then use one or more of these for comparison purposes with *Roe-Deer*.

## SUBJECT MATTER AND THEMES

*Mirror* has both a literal and metaphorical meaning in the poem. Like Hughes's poem it uses the concept of the relationship between reality and imagination. This can be represented in several ways, one of which is a reflection in a pool of water, or a glass, or a window. In the first stanza of the poem Plath describes herself through the thoughts and feelings of a mirror on the wall. In the second stanza the idea of the reflected image becomes more complex. Plath describes herself (the mirror) as a lake into which she looks, searching in the reflections, it seems, for her true self. This poem can be described as 'confessional', as Plath reveals the secret fears of her life.

The main themes of the poem include loneliness, unfaithfulness, and deception. The mirror and reflected water both represent the division between reality and imagination. The fear of old age and loss of youthful beauty rises up at the end of the poem.

## TONE, LANGUAGE, AND IMAGERY

The poem begins with the tone of a detached observer, but moves through darker emotions ending in fear of old age. This detached tone is at odds with the emotions that lie beneath the surface.

Like *Roe-Deer*, *Mirror* has some memorable images. Look at the image in the first stanza of the 'little god, four cornered'. The second stanza has more powerful images, with the most chilling being the final one in which Plath describes her youth being drowned and old age rising out of the 'lake', 'like a terrible fish'.

## STRUCTURE AND FORM

The poem is in two stanzas, each of nine lines. It has no regular line length or any rhyme pattern. Each stanza opens with a short sentence and there is a mixture of short and longer run-on sentences. The short sentences help give the superficially detached tone.

## COMPARISONS

*Mirror* could be compared with several poems from the selection. The theme of personal relationships could be compared with any of: *Long Distance*, *The Sick Equation*, *Blackberrying*, *Once Upon a Time*, *My Grandmother*, or *Afternoons*.

For the use of striking imagery, you could compare: *I Shall Return*, *Blackberrying*, *Churning Day*, *War Photographer*, *A Martian Sends a Postcard Home*, *Bedtime Story*, *An Advancement of Learning*, *Once Upon a Time*, *My Grandmother*, *Afternoons*, or *Roe-Deer*.

# POST-1914 POETRY

## *Harrison, Larkin, Patten, Jennings*

> *Before beginning this unit, go back to pages 36–37 and read again what examiners are looking for in an essay about post-1914 poetry.*

In this unit we will first study *Long Distance* by Tony Harrison and *Afternoons* by Philip Larkin.

The five aspects of the poems with which we are concerned are:

- subject
- mood and tone
- analysis of imagery/language
- form and structure
- theme

The question you will be asked on poetry requires a *comparison* to be made between two or more poems. You will be expected to respond to all the aspects noted above, but the most marks will be given for presenting a *comparative analysis* of thematic meaning and language.

## SUBJECT MATTER

|  | Long Distance | Afternoons | Points of comparison/contrast |
|---|---|---|---|
| Who is in the poem? | This is a personal poem about the poet's mother and father. The poet's presence is strong throughout the poem and central in the final stanza. | The poet is observing the 'new recreation ground' where young mothers have brought their children. Their husbands – skilled tradesmen – are mentioned, as are their 'courting-places'. Lovers – still at school – use the place as they once did before their weddings and children. |  |
| How does the poet speak to the reader? | The poem is personal and reflective. The poet is addressing the reader using the first person, but also uses second- and third-person forms. |  | The poems have very different levels of personal involvement. Both poets explore the feelings of people and their relationships, but Harrison is centrally involved in his poem, whereas Larkin is not. |

| | Long Distance | Afternoons | Points of comparison/contrast |
|---|---|---|---|
| Where and when is it set? | | It is an everyday working-class scene. The poem was written in 1959. Larkin lived in Hull but the scene could be anywhere. | |
| What is the poem about? | The first three stanzas explain that, although his mother had been dead for two years, his father was unable to accept her death. 'He *knew* she'd just popped out to get the tea'. In the final stanza we learn that the poet later feels the same about his parents' deaths. | | The poems are reflective rather than active. The passing of time is a common theme. People do ordinary things in each poem, for different reasons – warming slippers, taking the kids to the play area. |
| What are the most significant events/ characters? | | The ordinariness of the scene and the observation of real lives is significant. The mothers know that time is passing, 'pushing them/To the side of their own lives.' | A realization comes in the last stanza of each poem, to do with time and the changes it brings. |

## WRITING ACTIVITIES

1 Make a table like the one above, and fill in the gaps.
2 Prepare a short written or spoken presentation which explores the similarities and contrasts between the poems in terms of their subject matter.

# FORM AND STRUCTURE

## STRUCTURE AND FORM OF *Long Distance*

The overall structure of the poem presents one subject for the first three quatrains, which allows for introductory, developmental, and repeated ideas to be presented. These are concerned with the father's thoughts and feelings about the mother. The fourth quatrain is different. It is concerned with the poet's thoughts and feelings about his (now dead) parents.

## DISCUSSION ACTIVITY

Discuss, in pairs or small groups, the way Harrison has structured the ideas in his poem as suggested above.

The metre and rhyme scheme of the poem have been carefully constructed. It is essentially a pentameter (lines with five feet), with

some variation in lines one and three of the first stanza, and in the last
stanza.

> ### WRITING ACTIVITY
>
> 1 Write out the second stanza leaving a space between each line. Mark a vertical
> line after every two syllables. What do you find? Now do the same for each of
> the stanzas.

As well as this regularity of syllables, there is also a discernible
regularity to the 'stress' of the words.

> ### WRITING ACTIVITIES
>
> 2 Using the second stanza which you wrote out for Activity 1, put a cross above
> the syllables which you might accent or draw out as you read. Is there a pattern?
> 3 Now notate the rhyme scheme for the poem. What is interesting about the last
> stanza? Why is it like this, do you think?

## STRUCTURE AND FORM OF *Afternoons*

In this three-stanza poem, as with Harrison's, the ideas are developed
as the poem progresses. The scene is set and described in the first
stanza; in the second, the lives of the mothers are further revealed and
the 'ruining' of their former 'courting-places' is mentioned. In the
final stanza, more reflective ideas about what has happened to the
mothers' beauty, and what is happening to their lives, are presented.

Unlike Harrison's, there is no formal metrical structure or rhyme
scheme in Larkin's poem.

> ### WRITING ACTIVITY
>
> 4 Write a short description of the differences in structure and form of these two
> poems.

# MOOD OR TONE

The tone of a poem is the mood it conveys or the mood it evokes in
the reader. Put another way, the mood of a poem is established by the
tone of the words and ideas used.

Here are some random adjectives which might be applied to poems.

| bleak | solemn | sentimental | cold | warm | serious |
| light-hearted | fearsome | threatening | humorous | flippant | horrific |
| cynical | dismissive | patronizing | emotional | subjective | evil |
| detached | objective | erotic | exciting | sinister | respectful |
| ironic | satirical | tearful | reflective | | |

Note that the tone or mood of a poem may change as it progresses.

### WRITING ACTIVITY

Write down the words from the table above which you think apply to each of the poems. Then think of some more of your own. Apply different words to different parts of the poems if relevant.

Find quotations to support your choices, and explain them for each poem.

# THEMES

The 'theme' of a poem – or any other piece of writing – is what it is really about, apart from the events which happen and the people who make the events happen.

There is usually a point being made, an underlying meaning to the poem, as well as its surface narrative.

As you did with the subject matter, you need to be able to compare and contrast the poems. Here are some key words to help you do this.

| Long Distance | Afternoons | Both poems |
| --- | --- | --- |
| death | escape | loss |
| love | | class |
| not forgetting | | time passing |
| mourning | | family |
| after-life | | memories |

## THEMES OF *Long Distance*

### Death

Death is clearly a theme in the poem. The father cannot come to terms with the death of the mother. His actions, in effect pretending she is still alive, are described in the first two stanzas. Later, with the passing of time, we learn that the father has died also and the son describes his difficulty in accepting the death of his parents – he still calls the 'disconnected number'. The title *Long Distance* connects the image

of the impossible telephone call with the idea of the parents being a long way off, in a different world.

## Love

The love felt by the father for his wife is indicated by his caring actions and his sense of loss. Later, the poet seems to feel the same loss, which indicates a close, loving family. The warmth and cosiness of the domestic scene also reinforce the closeness of the parents and the family as a whole.

## Mourning and not forgetting

There is no overt mourning in the poem, but the father's actions are a kind of mourning. He not only does not forget his wife but he acts as if she is still there – it is almost irrational. Harrison emphasizes that 'he *knew* she'd just popped out to get the tea'. The son's disbelief is described as a 'blight'; as if his lack of belief was the abnormal behaviour.

### WRITING ACTIVITIES

1 Read the last stanza of the poem carefully. What does it say about belief in the after-life?

2 With selected quotations to support your views, note the themes you find in *Long Distance*.

## THEMES OF *Afternoons*

The poem shares many thematic ideas with *Long Distance*. However, the idea of 'escape' and 'freedom', or the lack of these, seems special to the poem. The mothers bring their children to the recreation ground for 'setting free'. Perhaps this freedom is from their living environment – the housing estate full of 'washing', and the confined life of small rooms and television. But the mothers themselves lack freedom and escape. Their lives now are predetermined, and they know what is 'behind them' and 'before them'. 'Their beauty has thickened' and something is taking over the centre of their lives and 'pushing' them to the side.

### WRITING ACTIVITY

3 Explain how the recreation ground is a symbol for freedom and escape. In what ways have the mothers lost their freedom? Explore the ideas in the last stanza in relation to this theme.

## THEMES OF BOTH POEMS

### Loss, memories, family

In *Afternoons*, these themes of loss, memories, and family are connected to 'escape and freedom'. The mothers have lost their independence and gained husbands and children. They are no longer the lovers in the park – they've lost that place to younger people. But they remember their 'courting-places' as, presumably, they remember 'their beauty'. The loss in *Long Distance* is loss of partner and then parents through death. The memories are kept alive for the husband by his ritual of maintaining his wife's habits. For the poet it is the 'leather phone book' which carries the memory of his parents. Both poems look back, and each is family-centred. We have a clear picture of the husbands and homes, and these are not disparaged by the poet nor by the mothers. Family homes are represented affectionately by the poets.

### Class

The poems are not overtly class-conscious, but both contexts are working class; phrases such as 'slippers warming by the gas', 'hot water bottles her side of the bed', 'her transport pass' evoke an everyday, working-class home environment. Also, 'husbands in skilled trades', 'an estateful of washing', and wedding albums 'near the television' evoke a similar scene. The ordinariness of the setting for each poem is a strength because it moves on to more complex ideas.

### Time passing

The two poems might be seen as a continuum. Some time in the future, one of the 'skilled trades' husbands may be mourning the loss of his wife in a poem written by one of the children. Previously, the wedding photographs of the husband and wife in *Long Distance* could have sat near the television.

In *Afternoons*, 'Summer is fading', and this symbolizes the passing of time for the mothers. In *Long Distance*, some years pass through the duration of the poem. *Long Distance* has a strong sense of closure because 'life ends with death' and both parents die. In *Afternoons*, there is no closure. There are many years of destiny in front of the young mothers – though with fewer choices.

## WRITING ACTIVITY

4 Paying close attention to the text of the poems, pick out some interesting similarities and contrasts in the themes of *Afternoons* and *Long Distance*.

# LANGUAGE AND IMAGERY

## IMAGERY AND LANGUAGE IN *Long Distance*

The poem is accessible because it describes an ordinary domestic situation, even if the actions are unusual.

> ### WRITING ACTIVITIES
>
> 1 Quote the 'ordinary' phrases from the first two stanzas and explain how readers would feel 'at home' with the poem.
> 2 What does the line 'To clear away her things and look alone' mean?

The phrase 'blight of disbelief' is the most complex idea in the poem. It refers to the father being sensitive to the son's rational view of death, and his fear that perhaps the son will force him to face the fact of his wife's death.

> ### WRITING ACTIVITY
>
> 3 Explain the meaning and appropriateness of the word 'blight'. What does the line tell you about the relationship between father and son?

'He'd hear her key scrape in the rusted lock and end his grief' combines a physical description – the lock – with a psychological one, of grief.

> ### WRITING ACTIVITIES
>
> 4 Explain in a paragraph the full effect and meaning of the line and how the ideas connect with the themes of the poem.
> 5 Explain how the phrases '*Long Distance*' and 'disconnected number' are used as related images in the poem.

## IMAGERY AND LANGUAGE IN *Afternoons*

There is a feeling of emptiness and loss in the poem.

> ### WRITING ACTIVITY
>
> 6 Discuss the above idea in relation to the following phrases used by Larkin:
>    - 'Summer is fading'
>    - 'The leaves fall in ones and twos'
>    - 'In the hollows of afternoons'
>    - 'the wind/Is ruining their courting-places'
>    - 'Something is pushing them/To the side of their own lives'

> ## ESSAY QUESTIONS: 'LONG DISTANCE' AND 'AFTERNOONS'
>
> 1  Choose two or three of the themes explored in both poems and show how each of the poets uses language to make his points effectively.
> 2  Show how the poets have used simple, everyday language and images to express quite complex ideas.

# The Sick Equation

In Brian Patten's poem a man looks back on the reasons why the 'sick' relationship between his parents caused him to spurn relationships of his own, until he realizes that he 'was wrong of course'. Each stanza deals with an aspect of his attitude and eventual realization.

## SUBJECT MATTER

| Stanza | Subject |
| --- | --- |
| 1<br>lines 1–11 | The voice of the poem is that of the poet writing in the first person. He remembers the certainties of school – the equation he learned and the 'teacher's cane'. He compares this to the 'anger and pain' of his unhappy home life, where there was less certainty. |
| 2 and 3<br>lines 12–23 | Believing that marriage, as in his parents' case, brought unhappiness, he turned his back on relationships, 'kept my head down low'. He thought of its possibilities but always with 'anguish'. |
| 4<br>lines 24–30 | Staying single, whenever he attended a wedding he 'saw the shadow . . . of divorce' fall over the bride and groom, despite their optimism. |
| 5<br>lines 31–37 | The poet finally changes. He realizes, albeit late in life, that just because some people's marriages fail doesn't mean everybody's will. The giving and taking of love will bring freedom. |

> ## ▍WRITING ACTIVITY
>
> 1  Which do you think is the most powerful or moving of the stanzas in the poem? Quote and explain.

## FORM AND STRUCTURE

The poem is personal and reflective and follows the natural patterns of speech. This does not mean that there is no rhythm to it. Natural speech patterns have rhythm, emphasis, and stress. Just by looking at the poem on the page, you can see that neither the overall structure, nor the length of lines are regular.

> ## ▍DISCUSSION ACTIVITY
>
> In pairs, copy out any four- or five-line section of the poem and mark 'stressed' and 'unstressed' symbols above the syllables. Discuss what you find.

Rhyme scheme

Analysis of the rhyme scheme will also prove more interesting than you might at first think.

**WRITING ACTIVITY**

2 Taking each stanza separately, notate the rhyme scheme. What do you find? Comment on the ways rhyme is used.

## MOOD OR TONE

The mood is *reflective*, *meditative*, and *thoughtful*. The poet is 'chewing over' the past and what he has learned – so it may be said to be '*ruminative*'. The poet is not bitter or angry because of his past. By the end of the poem he feels a satisfaction and a resolution to the problem of the sick equation, in his understanding of the importance of love.

There are also moments in the first three stanzas when the words convey a particular tone, e.g. 'raw', 'hate', 'anger', 'pain', 'stung'.

**WRITING ACTIVITY**

3 Find words in the other stanzas which suggest particular tones.
4 With reference to the words and phrases used by the poet, explain how the mood and tone of the poem reflects the seriousness of its subject matter.

## THEMES

The table below will allow you to cross-reference themes from the three poems in this unit so far. Look back at the previous section on 'Themes' (page 74) and compare.

| Themes in *Sick Equation* | Notes |
|---|---|
| Disharmony/order | The poet found disharmony and lack of order in his family because of the poor relationship between his parents. This contrasted with the certainty, 'engraved in stone', of the equation 1+1 = 2. The first stanza explores this. |
| Self-worth | *What do stanzas 2 and 3 say about the poet's feeling of inadequacy?* |
| Commitment | The idea of commitment was a sour one for the poet, full of difficulties. , He worried for those he saw making commitments at weddings, always believing that divorce would be the outcome. |
| Solitariness | *In what ways was the poet 'singular'? What effect did this have on him?* |
| Love | Love is the major theme of the poem. There is lack of love, or fractured love, in the beginning, followed by the realization that only through love can true relationships be formed, and the sick equation made whole. |

## LANGUAGE AND IMAGERY

The poem is built on the image which forms its title. The equation 1+1=2, which is sure and safe in mathematics, becomes uncertain and 'sick' when the components are people, not numbers.

In the first stanza the mathematical equation could be 'engraved in stone', it is an 'absolute' that the poet 'could not question or refute'.

In stanzas 3 and 4 (lines 16–30) Patten uses an extended image of 'flight'. The key words are:

'kept my head down low'          'drifted'
'dreams of flight'                'weighed down'
'flightless'                      'flight's an anguish'
'albatross'                       'dreams of flying free'

# My Grandmother

In *My Grandmother* by Elizabeth Jennings, the voice of the poem is in the first person. The poet is thinking back on the life of her grandmother and, particularly, an incident when she 'refused/To go out with her'.

## THEMES

The table on the next page will allow you to cross-reference themes from the four poems in this unit. Look back at the previous sections on 'Themes' (pages 74 and 79) and compare.

| Themes in *My Grandmother* | Notes |
|---|---|
| Relationships | We have the impression that the grandmother may not have been good at forming relationships – except with her antiques. |
| Loneliness | *How is the loneliness of the grandmother represented in stanza 3?* |
| Possessions | The antique possessions are detailed in the poem. They seem to have been the grandmother's obsession – 'She kept an antique shop – or it kept her.' |
| Age/time passing | *Give an account of the movement of time and people's ages as the poem progresses.* |
| Death | Antiques belong to a time which has passed – to people already dead. Death seems to haunt the grandmother in her love of dead things, her protection of them in 'one long, narrow room', in her frailty and ultimately in her own death. |
| Love | The poet shows a lack of love for her grandmother when she refuses to go out with her. The grandmother herself lacks love, preferring polish. She seems to have self-love – 'She watched her own reflection. . .' |
| Rejection | *Each of the two characters suffers rejection in the poem. Explain how this is so.* |
| Guilt | For the poet, grief is replaced by guilt when her grandmother dies. She feels her grandmother's life was misdirected – towards things 'she never used', things which offered her no love. But the young girl withheld her love on that guilty occasion. |

## WRITING ACTIVITIES

1 Answer the questions in the table.
2 Decide which of the themes suggested for *My Grandmother* apply to the other poems studied in this unit.

## LANGUAGE AND IMAGERY

There is a contrast in the language and tone between stanza 1 and stanza 3.

The detail in stanza 1 is lively and colourful, 'Apostle spoons', 'Bristol glass', 'brass', 'Salvers and silver bowls'.

The key words in stanza 3 are not lively – they are connected with death. Everything smells 'old'; the long, narrow room reminds the reader of a tomb; there is a 'smell of absences'. The grandmother has become a ghost of her previous self, a ghost which does not 'give her own reflection back again'.

## WRITING ACTIVITY

3 Contrast the language, imagery, and tone of stanzas 1 and 3, quoting phrases from the poem.

# EXAMINATION QUESTIONS

With the paragraphs you have prepared in the activities above, you are now ready to put together an essay to answer an English Literature examination question. The question might be like one of the following:

> **Question 1:** In the poem *Long Distance* by Tony Harrison, the poet writes about family relationships. Compare the poem with one other from the post-1914 section of *Best Words* in which the poet also explores the theme of family relationships.
>
> **Question 2:** Compare *Afternoons* by Philip Larkin with one other poem from the post-1914 selection of *Best Words* that uses descriptions of scenes to bring the poem alive.

For Question 1 you could use *Afternoons* to answer the question, or *The Sick Equation*, *I Shall Return*, *Churning Day*, *Once Upon A Time*, or *My Grandmother*.

For Question 2 on descriptions of scenes you could use *Long Distance*, or *I Shall Return*, *Blackberrying*, *Churning Day*, *War Photographer*, *Bedtime Story*, *An Advancement of Learning*, *Once Upon A Time*, *Mirror*, *My Grandmother*, or *Roe-Deer*.

You can see that both questions leave you the option to choose different poems. The question will not be a closed one that you can only answer with two specific poems. There will be scope for a choice of several poems in your comparison.

Remember that the key words of the question are the starting point for your answer. In Question 1, these are: **explores the theme of family relationships**. In Question 2, they are: **descriptions of scenes to bring the poem alive**. Keep your answer focused on the key words, but bring in other closely connected aspects if possible.

# INTRODUCTION TO PROSE

This section of the book will help you study the novel you are reading for your end-of-course examination so that, when the time comes, you will feel confident that you know the book well enough to tackle any question.

## WHAT WILL THE EXAMINERS EXPECT OF ME?

First of all, you need to demonstrate your **knowledge** of the novel – the story line(s), characters, setting, etc. However, this does not mean that they want you to re-tell the story. The examiners have read it more than once! They want you to use your knowledge *selectively*, picking out relevant aspects that will help you to answer the question.

The writing activities and exam-type questions in this book will guide you in the right direction. Above all, you must focus closely on the question. Identify the **key words** and make sure that they are central to your essay plan.

## WHAT KNOWLEDGE AND UNDERSTANDING DO I NEED?

Examiners often set questions based on the **characters**. You need to know:

- facts – appearance, physical features, etc.
- personality – what makes them tick
- behaviour – what they do and how they react
- relationships
- how others react towards them
- whether they change in any way, and why.

A character-based essay has to be more than a list of points; you need to be able to explain how you know about the character – what proof you have. Writers give clues, particularly when a character appears for the first time. This section of your *Students' Book* will show you how to track characters as you read the novel, helping you to build up a set of notes and quotations.

Your answers may focus on characters, but must be linked to one or more of the following aspects:

- the structure of the novel
- the words and actions of the characters
- how characters' actions relate to themes (such as marriage in *Wuthering Heights* and nature in *Far From the Madding Crowd*)
- the language used by the writers and its effectiveness
- relationships between characters
- the extent to which readers sympathize with characters
- selective reference to the cultural and historical background of the novel.

Very often, the **setting** of a novel is vital, as is the **atmosphere**. Look out for descriptions, as suggested in the following units, and notice how the atmosphere may change according to events, and how it may be in tune with the action.

Be aware of the **narrator**. Who is telling the story? What **viewpoint** is being presented? Is the story being told through the eyes of an all-seeing, neutral third person, who is not one of the characters, or is one of the characters telling the story, thus presenting a one-sided, first-person narrative? Does the viewpoint change at all?

Think about any message that the writer is trying to convey through the characters and events. What are the main **themes** of the novel? What does it make you think about? How does it make you feel? Why?

**Remember:** Always look carefully at the examination question. What are the key words? What, exactly, are you being asked to write about? Focus on these words, and write about what you are asked. Then the examiner will be able to give the best possible marks for all the knowledge and understanding you show when answering the question.

# WUTHERING HEIGHTS

## *Emily Brontë*

> *Before beginning this unit, go back to pages 83–84 and read again what examiners are looking for in an essay about pre-1914 prose.*

## BACKGROUND AND CONTEXT

Emily Brontë was born in Yorkshire in 1818, the daughter of a very traditional Church of England clergyman. She had several siblings, but only her sisters Charlotte and Anne and her brother Branwell survived into adulthood. Their mother died and the children's aunt came to live with them on the Yorkshire Moors – the setting for *Wuthering Heights*. Their home, Haworth Parsonage, was in a very remote and exposed area of the countryside, causing the children to lead a rather isolated existence. They used their active imaginations to create their own fantasy worlds – the beginning of a story-telling habit for the Brontës.

Emily Brontë spent a short time away teaching, but returned to Haworth because she missed the life there so much. She died at Haworth in 1848, aged only 29.

### RESEARCH ACTIVITIES

Find out about some of the following:
+ Charlotte Brontë
+ Anne Brontë
+ The children's schooldays
+ Their father and brother
+ Emily's life as a teacher
+ Haworth

## PLOT

The action of *Wuthering Heights* moves between two houses on the Yorkshire Moors – Wuthering Heights and Thrushcross Grange.

The Earnshaw family, including two children called Hindley and Catherine, live at Wuthering Heights. Their life is turned upside down by the arrival of a homeless child of about the same age as Catherine.

Named Heathcliff, he is brought back from Liverpool by old Mr Earnshaw after a business trip. His aim is to bring the waif up as one of his own, but this causes resentment among his family. Catherine and Heathcliff became friends, but Hindley is jealous of him.

When old Mr Earnshaw dies, his son, Hindley, bullies Heathcliff mercilessly and encourages Catherine to become friendly with Edgar Linton. Hindley becomes more of a cruel bully after his wife Frances dies giving birth to their son, Hareton. After Heathcliff overhears Catherine say that he is not good enough for her to marry, he disappears.

Catherine later marries the rather weak and insipid Edgar. When Heathcliff finally returns he marries Edgar's sister Isabella, but is very cruel in his treatment of her. He still loves Catherine, who dies in childbirth. The baby – a girl named Cathy – survives.

Heathcliff is particularly unkind to Hindley in revenge for the way he was treated when they were younger. Isabella escapes after a fight between Heathcliff and Hindley. She lives near London, and gives birth to a son, Linton. Hindley dies about six months after Catherine.

Years later, Heathcliff virtually forces his son Linton to marry Cathy, and after Edgar's death Heathcliff claims ownership of the Grange as well as the Heights. Linton dies. Heathcliff rents the Grange to Lockwood.

Heathcliff by now longs to die so that he can be reunited with Catherine. He expects Cathy to marry Hareton and so unite the houses of Wuthering Heights and Thrushcross Grange.

| | | Mr Earnshaw | m. | Mrs Earnshaw | | | Mr Linton | | m. | | Mrs Linton |
|---|---|---|---|---|---|---|---|---|---|---|---|
| | | d Oct 1777 | | d spring 1773 | | | d Oct 1780 | | | | |
| Frances | m. | Hindley | | Catherine | m. | | Edgar | Isabella | m. | | Heathcliff |
| d 1778 | | b summer 1757 | | b summer 1765 | | | b 1762 | b 1765 | | | b 1764 |
| | | d Sept 1784 | | d March 1784 | 1783 | | d Sept 1801 | d summer 1797 | | | d May 1802 |
| Hareton | | | m. | Cathy | | | | m. | | | Linton |
| b June 1778 | | | 1 Jan 1803 | b March 1784 | | | | Sept 1801 | | | b Sept 1784 |
| | | | | | | | | | | | d 1801 |

It is a good idea to be quite sure you know who is who and the relationship between the various characters. The family tree on page 86 should help.

### WRITING ACTIVITY

Using the information in the family tree, draw a time-line from 1773 to 1803. Add the significant births, marriages, and deaths, and any other key events you can place. For example, at the end of Chapter 9 we are told that in 1783 Ellen moved from Wuthering Heights to Thrushcross Grange.

The plot is in fact relatively straightforward, but it is complicated by Brontë's use of several narrators and a somewhat complex time scheme.

The novel begins in 1801 – look at the details on the family tree to see what happened in that year. At first, the narrator is Mr Lockwood, who has rented Thrushcross Grange from its owner, the rather morose Heathcliff, who lives at Wuthering Heights. Lockwood decides to visit his landlord, but a snowstorm forces him to stay the night, during which he is disturbed by the dream of a child begging to be let in. He talks about this to Ellen Dean, the housekeeper. She then becomes the narrator and tells the story, from the arrival of Heathcliff in the house, up to the death of Linton in September 1801.

Lockwood returns to Thrushcross Grange in 1802 and finds that Heathcliff is dead and Cathy is now the lover of Hareton. He passes the grave of Catherine, which lies between the graves of Edgar and Heathcliff. There have been rumours that the ghosts of Catherine and Heathcliff have been seen on the moors.

## SETTING

The novel is set mainly in the two houses – Wuthering Heights and Thrushcross Grange, and on the moors that separate them.

In Chapter 20, the young Linton asks 'Is Wuthering Heights as pleasant a place as Thrushcross Grange?'

Ellen lives and works in both houses and so has an intimate knowledge of both – the atmosphere, people, and life. She tells Linton that Wuthering Heights is 'not so buried in trees' and says the air there is 'fresher and dryer'. This positive description also hints at the Heights being more exposed to the moors and the elements. In contrast, Thrushcross Grange is in a valley and so it is more sheltered.

The physical setting of the two houses reflects the characters, events, and emotions within. The sheltered Grange is  home to the over-protected Linton children. The Heights, in contrast, is where the passionate and highly emotional characters live.

Heathcliff and Catherine 'rebel' by leaving the 'shivering corners' of the Heights to see the Grange, a 'splendid place carpeted with crimson, and crimson-covered chairs and tables, and a pure white ceiling bordered by gold, a shower of glass-drops hanging in silver chains from the centre and shimmering with little soft tapers'. The difference is immense and is underlined by Brontë's use of descriptive language which is gentler, softer, and richer than her descriptions of the Heights.

> ## ▌WRITING ACTIVITY
>
> Design a chart on which you can keep track of the events that take place in the two houses. It is probably best to make this chronological. Head your columns:
>
> **Year    House    Event    Characters involved    Atmosphere**
>
> This exercise should help you write about the differences between the two houses, and what goes on in them.

The two houses are separated by four miles of inhospitable moors, which provide a physical and atmospheric barrier.

When Lockwood makes his second journey to the Heights, the elements seem to be determined to trap him as he arrives 'just in time to escape the first feathery flakes of snow.' Notice the softness of this sentence, compared to the harshness of the next: 'On that bleak hill-top, the earth was hard with a black frost.'

The inhospitability of the people at the Heights is echoed and emphasized by the references to the weather, even though the fire is apparently welcoming. The weather worsens, there is a 'bitter whirl of wind and suffocating snow'.

Brontë frequently uses the pathetic fallacy (where the weather provides a sympathetic background) in *Wuthering Heights*.

◆ Lockwood's dream comes against a background of 'driving snow'.

◆ The night Heathcliff disappears is one of 'violent wind, as well as thunder'.

◆ Isabella's escape from the Heights is conducted against a background of 'writhing drifts'.

## WRITING ACTIVITY

Build up a list of important events in the lives of the characters, and add details of the weather and atmosphere on the moors at the time they happen.

## ESSAY QUESTION: SETTING

Examine the extent to which Brontë uses setting and atmosphere to increase the drama of the action.

# CHARACTERS

Examiners often focus questions on one or more of the characters. They may ask, for example: *Does Hindley deserve to die a penniless drunk?*

Your answer would need to include, among other things, consideration of the way his life is changed when Heathcliff arrives, his relationship with his father and sister, his marriage and the effect of his wife's death, his treatment of Heathcliff and Hareton, and his gambling.

On the other hand, the question may ask you to compare characters. For example: *Do you feel more sympathy for Isabella or Edgar?*

In this case, you would need to consider why – if at all – they deserve sympathy. This could be because of their upbringing, their relationships, how they behave, what they do, what others do that affects them, and what finally happens to them. You would then need to make a choice!

## CHARACTER TRACKING

All character questions expect you to show that you can write about appearance (and what this suggests about their personality), behaviour, and relationships. It is therefore important that you build up a comprehensive set of notes and quotations on the characters so that you can write confidently about any of them. To do this, you need to keep track of when they appear or are mentioned. Notice what is going on and look for key words that give clues.

## HEATHCLIFF

We first see Heathcliff through Lockwood's eyes. He is described as a 'solitary' character with 'black eyes' who reluctantly invites Lockwood in – this reluctance being shown by the way he speaks 'with closed teeth'. Heathcliff is described as a 'dark skinned gypsy' with 'the manners of a gentleman' and 'a degree of underpride'. Adjectives such as 'surly', 'morose', and 'slovenly' add to the picture we have of him. He seems almost pleased that his dogs go for Lockwood, as they 'do right to be vigilant', and he relaxes and offers him a glass of wine. However, when Lockwood leaves, Heathcliff 'evidently wished no repetition of my intrusion'.

### WRITING ACTIVITY

1  Given the chance, what would you ask Heathcliff? Write down several questions then discuss them with a partner and try to answer each other's questions.

Heathcliff's introduction in Chapter 1 serves to make us curious – as it does Lockwood. Lockwood returns to Wuthering Heights the next day and is again treated inhospitably. He notices the relationship Heathcliff has with Cathy and Hareton, and this gives us more insight into his character. He 'demanded' that Cathy make the tea, and speaks so 'savagely' that he reveals 'a genuine bad nature'. His moment of relaxation the previous day now seems to be out of character, particularly when he says 'I don't keep accommodations for visitors'.

Chapter 3 gives details of Lockwood's nightmares. We have already been told that Heathcliff 'had an odd notion about the chamber' where Lockwood stays and 'would never let anybody lodge there willingly'. Heathcliff's reaction to Lockwood's yell adds to the many unanswered questions about him. As Lockwood leaves the room, Heathcliff 'wrenched open the lattice, bursting, as he pulled it, into an uncontrollable passion of tears'.

The following day, Heathcliff is again morose and bad tempered. It becomes apparent that he often hits Cathy, as she springs 'to a safer distance' when he raises his hand. He does, however, escort Lockwood back to the Grange.

### WRITING ACTIVITIES

2  Produce a list of adjectives that could be used to describe Heathcliff. Include physical details as well as personality and behaviour. Find quotations to support your choices, then compare your list with a partner's.

> 3 Write a paragraph to describe the Heathcliff of the first three chapters. What
> unanswered questions are there?

Lockwood is curious – hence his questioning of Ellen Dean. Her
narrative gives the reader some understanding of Heathcliff's
personality and behaviour, even if it does not excuse it.

Track through Chapter 4, noting what happens to the young
Heathcliff. Find the evidence for the following:

- In Liverpool, he was apparently a homeless waif.
- When old Mr Earnshaw brings him to Wuthering
  Heights, he is 'a dirty, ragged, black-haired child'.
- He is clearly frightened.
- They talk about him as if he were an object, calling
  him 'it'.
- Hindley is upset as his violin is broken – and he
  blames Heathcliff.
- Mr Earnshaw has lost Catherine's present, and she spits
  Heathcliff.
- He becomes friends with Catherine, but Hindley resents
  him and often beats him.
- Ellen Dean is unkind to him.
- He never complains about these beatings but knows he
  could use them to his advantage.
- He seems to be ungrateful.

## WRITING ACTIVITIES

4 Consider the Heathcliff that Lockwood meets in the first three chapters. Then
  go through the information from Chapter 4. How much of the older Heathcliff's
  behaviour and personality can now be understood?

5 What do you think about old Mr Earnshaw's decision to bring Heathcliff up as
  one of his own children? You may like to consider why Heathcliff is given that
  name.

6 Can Hindley's behaviour be justified?

Following his father's death, Hindley, who has been sent away to
college, returns with Frances – the wife no one knows about. He
quickly becomes 'tyrannical'. Remembering 'his old hatred of the
boy', he reduces Heathcliff to the condition of a servant who should
'labour out of doors'. So Heathcliff goes from being old Mr
Earnshaw's favourite to a common labourer. However, he bears 'his
degradation pretty well'.

## WRITING ACTIVITIES

**7** Track through Chapter 6, focusing in particular on what Heathcliff says and does, and on how he is treated by Hindley and Catherine. Consider the way this treatment might have affected him. Key points to consider include:

♦ Heathcliff's second-hand education by Catherine

♦ Heathcliff and Catherine's promise to 'grow up as rude as savages'

♦ their visit to Thrushcross Grange – what they see of the house and the behaviour of its inhabitants

♦ what the Lintons say about Heathcliff after he and Catherine are caught.

**8** Catherine's return from the Grange five weeks later clearly affects Heathcliff. Find the passages that show:

♦ her changed appearance and manner

♦ Hindley's enjoyment of Heathcliff's 'discomfiture'

♦ Heathcliff's objection to being laughed at

♦ his behaviour at Christmas

♦ his reaction to the arrival of the Linton children

♦ his treatment of Edgar.

Notice the way Heathcliff moves between control and subservience. How does this help you to understand him?

## WRITING ACTIVITY

**9** Consider Heathcliff's comment: 'I'm trying to settle how I shall pay Hindley back. I don't care how long I wait, if I can only do it, at last. I hope he will not die before I do!' What are the implications of this statement, and how do they affect Heathcliff's behaviour later in the novel?

Chapter 8 begins with the birth of Hareton Earnshaw and the death of Frances. Hindley focuses his anger and grief on Heathcliff to such an extent that his treatment of Heathcliff is 'enough to make a fiend of a saint' and he becomes 'daily more notable for savage sullenness and ferocity'.

Heathcliff and Catherine remain friends, but he is upset by her rejection of him when Edgar visits.

In Chapter 9, he overhears Catherine say she has agreed to marry Edgar and that it would 'degrade' her to marry Heathcliff, but he doesn't hear her say: 'so he shall never know how I love him'. Heathcliff leaves the Heights and does not return for several years.

## WRITING ACTIVITY

**10** Who do you blame the most for Heathcliff's disappearance – Hindley, Catherine, or Heathcliff himself?

Continue tracking Heathcliff as you read through the rest of the novel. Look out for:

- what he says and does
- how others treat him
- what happens to him
- events that affect him.

Make notes of key words and quotations. You will no doubt include:

- Heathcliff's gambling with Hindley
- his fight with Edgar
- Isabella's infatuation and their elopement
- his treatment of Isabella after their return
- Catherine's death
- Hindley's death
- Isabella's escape
- Linton's arrival
- Edgar's death and burial
- Lockwood's visits and dreams.

Now consider Heathcliff's relationship with the other characters. Copy the character map below and complete it by adding Hareton, Isabella, Edgar, Cathy, and Linton. Write along the connecting lines a description of the relationship in each case.

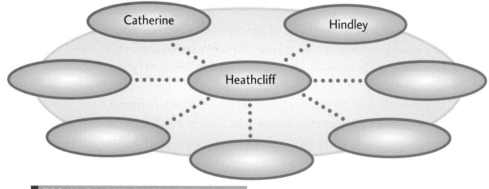

### ESSAY QUESTIONS: HEATHCLIFF

1 Write a character analysis of Heathcliff. Use quotations to support your points, and the notes you have made to guide you.

2 To what extent do you sympathize with Heathcliff? Consider the way he is treated by others, beginning with being 'adopted' by old Mr Earnshaw.

## CATHERINE

Lockwood's nightmare introduces us to Catherine Earnshaw, Catherine Linton, and Catherine Heathcliff – Earnshaw is her maiden name, Linton is her married name and Heathcliff is the name she most desires. This idea is supported by Heathcliff's reaction to the dream as it shows there is a close relationship between them. Lockwood's treatment of the apparition of the young child – 'I pulled its wrist onto the broken pane, and rubbed it to and fro till the blood ran down' – evokes our sympathy for Catherine.

As a six-year-old, Catherine is a confident and capable rider. She initially resents Heathcliff because her father has lost the riding whip he bought her, and she 'showed her humour by spitting at the stupid little thing'. However, after only a few days, 'Miss Cathy and he were now very thick'.

Ellen describes her as 'mischievous and wayward', 'a wild wick slip' with 'the bonniest eye.' Her high spirits are always in evidence.

**WRITING ACTIVITY**

11 Track carefully through Chapters 3 and 4, looking at Catherine's comments in her diary, and the things she says and does. Produce a list of key words to describe her. Find quotations to support your choices, and compare your list with a partner's. Write a paragraph to describe Catherine at this point.

Continue to track the character of Catherine, noting in particular her influence on events and on other characters. You will need to consider:

- her behaviour on the night of her father's death (Chapter 5)
- her reaction when peering into Thrushcross Grange (Chapter 6)
- her changed behaviour after her return (Chapter 7)
- her treatment of Heathcliff (Chapter 7)
- her rejection of Heathcliff when Edgar visits (Chapter 8)
- her reasons for marrying Edgar not Heathcliff (Chapters 7 & 9)
- her responsibility for Heathcliff's disappearance (Chapter 9).

**WRITING ACTIVITY**

12 What is your assessment of Catherine? To what extent do you feel sorry for her? Given the chance, what would you like to ask her? Write down several questions, then compare them with a partner's and try to answer each other's questions.

Continue to track Catherine up to her death, noticing in particular:

- her reaction to Heathcliff's return (Chapter 10)
- her refusal to accept the blame for anything (Chapters 11 & 15)
- her determination to have her own way (Chapter 11)
- her assumption that everyone likes her (Chapter 12)
- the way she makes herself ill (Chapter 15).

> **ESSAY QUESTION: CATHERINE**
>
> Write a character analysis of Catherine Earnshaw/Linton, using your notes to help. Use quotations to support your points.

Character map

To consider the relationships between Catherine and others, produce a character map like the one on page 93, with Catherine in the middle. Add Ellen, Edgar, Heathcliff, Hareton, Hindley, and Mr Earnshaw. Connect the characters and write along the connecting lines a description of the relationship between them.

# THEMES

Perhaps the main theme of *Wuthering Heights* is **love**, but does this mean it is a love story? Are any of the relationships happy? Do any survive? Catherine and Heathcliff are obsessed with one another, but their relationship never matures. Several marriages take place – Hindley and Frances, Catherine and Edgar, Heathcliff and Isabella, Cathy and Linton, Cathy and Hareton.

> **WRITING ACTIVITIES**
>
> **1** For each of these marriages consider:
> - why did they marry?
> - was the marriage a happy one?
> - how did it end?
> - was there any real love within the marriage?
>
> **2** Are there any happy marriages in *Wuthering Heights*? Include reference to several of the marriages and write about the characters involved and the way they treated each other as well as their reasons for marrying.

Other themes for you to consider include the following:

## THE SUPERNATURAL

Catherine's ghost is mentioned several times after Lockwood's nightmare. Ellen talks of Heathcliff's ghost haunting the moors. There are also references to witches. Find the references to the supernatural and consider their effect on action, behaviour, and atmosphere.

## DEATH

The death of a character has a profound effect on those who survive. Heathcliff, for example, suffers at the hands of Hindley following old Mr Earnshaw's death. Go back to the family tree on page 86 to remind yourself of the number of deaths. Consider the circumstances of each.

## IMPRISONMENT

This idea includes an emotional sense of being imprisoned as well as the physical idea of being trapped. At the beginning, Lockwood is trapped at the Heights by the weather, and then is trapped in the coffin-like bed where he dreams of Catherine's ghost. Emotionally, Heathcliff is trapped by his obsession for Catherine. In contrast, the young Catherine and Heathcliff often run away over the moors to experience a sense of freedom. Find other examples of characters being trapped or trying to escape.

## WINDOWS

The ghost of Catherine tries to get in through a window and Heathcliff is found dead by the same window. She and Heathcliff first see the Linton children through a window, and when Heathcliff returns, Catherine and Edgar are by an open window. Find other instances where windows are important, and consider the significance of these.

## SOCIAL CLASS

Catherine cannot marry Heathcliff because it would 'degrade' her. Hindley treats Heathcliff like a servant, and the Lintons assume he is a 'villain'. Joseph is clearly of a lower class, which is illustrated by the way he talks. Lockwood assumes Hareton is a servant. Consider these judgements based on appearance and behaviour, to help you understand the importance of social class in the nineteenth century.

### EXAMINATION QUESTIONS

1 In her letter to Ellen, Isabella asks 'Is Mr Heathcliff a man? If so, is he mad? And if not, is he a devil?' How would you respond to this question?

2 To what extent do you consider Catherine to be the cause of most of the unhappiness?

3 Do you find the ending of *Wuthering Heights* a satisfactory one? Refer to characters and events in your answer.

4 In what ways does Chapter 1 prepare the reader for what happens later in the novel?

5 Analyse the character of Isabella. To what extent does she deserve the reader's sympathy?

6 What do we learn about Lockwood in the opening chapters? To what extent is he a reliable narrator? Justify your answer by referring to his words and actions.

7 To what extent is Cathy like her mother? You need to consider what they say and do, and how they behave, as well as comparing their personalities and backgrounds.

# FAR FROM THE MADDING CROWD

## *Thomas Hardy*

*Before beginning this unit, go back to pages 83–84 and read again what examiners are looking for in an essay about pre-1914 prose.*

## BACKGROUND AND CONTEXT

Thomas Hardy was born at Upper Bockhampton, Dorset in 1840 and died 88 years later, in 1928, at Dorchester, Dorset. He lived, therefore, through a period of great change, technological progress, and moral upheaval – as well as through a number of wars including a world war. Hardy was the son of a builder and master mason and, though not a physically strong child, enjoyed and progressed in his school work. The headmaster of his school aroused and encouraged in Hardy a love of the classical writers, which was to have a marked influence on his work. In 1856, he left school and became the pupil of an architect and church restorer. At this point in his life Hardy was reading widely and avidly with the thought of taking holy orders. Hardy worked as an architect in London for some time before returning to the west country. Work on the restoration of a church in Cornwall in 1870 led to his meeting Emma Gifford, sister-in-law of the rector. They married in 1874, the year of the publication of *Far From the Madding Crowd*. Hardy had enjoyed some success with three novels he had published since 1872 and, encouraged by his wife, gave up architecture for writing. They eventually settled at Max Gate, near Dorchester, where Hardy lived for the rest of his life.

Hardy had considerable success as a novelist and, later in his long life, as a poet. In 1910 he was awarded the Order of Merit. In 1912, Emma Hardy died. Although the marriage was not always very happy, Hardy was grief-stricken, as many of his later poems show. In 1914 Hardy married his secretary, who survived him and with him wrote his autobiography. Thomas Hardy died on 11 January 1928. His ashes were placed in Poet's Corner, Westminster Abbey and his heart was buried in the grave of his first wife at Stinsford, near his birthplace.

1    Find a time-line for Thomas Hardy which shows his movements and publications; note the extent of his writing.

2    Browse the following web sites:

www.stfx.ca/people/rnemesva/Hardy

education.guardian.co.uk/netclass/schools/english/links/0,5607,77240,00.html

3    Find and read some of the poems published after his first wife's death in 1912.

# SOCIAL AND HISTORICAL CONTEXT

In his Preface to a reprinting of *Far From the Madding Crowd*, Hardy writes about some aspects of rural life. Looking back from a time between 1895 and 1902, he recalls that it was in writing this novel that he first adopted the word 'Wessex'. He mentions some of the everyday features of his Wessex of 1874 under Queen Victoria. These included:

- Railways
- The Penny Post
- Mowing and reaping machines
- Union Workhouses
- Lucifer matches
- Labourers who could read and write
- National Schools

Hardy goes on to say that some of the aspects of everyday social life referred to in the novel have disappeared or changed. These include:

- 'divination by Bible and key' referred to by Liddy in Chapter 13
- the shearing supper, described in Chapter 23
- long smock frocks such as the one worn by Oak at his second attempt to get hired in Chapter 6
- the harvest-home
- the 'supplanting of stationary cottagers' by migratory workers.

The farm workers who make up the local, labouring class of the novel would have retained their cottages for life and even for generations. This situation was due to end by the turn of the century. Migratory workers – who moved from place to place, later accompanied by farm machinery – hired out their expertise and then moved on. As Hardy points out, this led to a break in the continuity of local history. It also led to the erosion or destruction of aspects of rural life as it was in 1874: folklore, close inter-social relations and the existence of eccentric individuals.

Hardy portrays local gossip to show the significance of any change in a rural community, and the inadequacies of that community. This is illustrated in Chapter 15, in Oak's conversation with the 'ancient man of malt'.

National and world events would not have had much impact in rural communities and there is no reference to them in the novel. The major events were the fairs and markets which required visits to larger towns: the Greenhill Sheep Fair is likened to Nijni Novgorod, the Russian city renowned for its huge fair held every August. The army journeying through town to or from its barracks would have been a reminder of a wider world. Troy evokes and manipulates the excitement attached to that. He spends time in America, but nobody else in the novel goes very far.

The title of the novel reflects these points. It comes from Gray's 'Elegy Written in a Country Churchyard':

Far from the madding crowd's ignoble strife
    Their sober wishes never learn'd to stray;
Along the cool, sequester'd vale of life
    They kept the noiseless tenor of their way.

## RESEARCH ACTIVITIES

1 Find out the extent to which railway communication had expanded by 1874.
2 What were the Penny Post and Lucifer matches?
3 Research the conditions of the Workhouse. Find out where the nearest one was to your locality.
4 Find out when the National Schools started and what kind of education was available in 1874.
5 What do the four lines from Gray's Elegy mean? How does this fit the novel?

## WRITING ACTIVITIES

1 Does the postal service work in Weatherbury? How do you know?
2 Find and read references to the Workhouse in the novel. For whom is this institution significant?
3 Read about, then explain 'divination by Bible and key' (see Chapter 13).
4 Describe the main details of the sheep-shearing and the supper that are obviously authentic representations of rural life.
5 Everyday social activities include gossip, weddings, church services, and going to the pub. Find and note significant references to these in the novel.

# SETTING AND PLOT

## SETTING

The novel is set in Wessex, which was the name of a kingdom in south-west England in Anglo-Saxon times, used by Thomas Hardy as the name of the county in which his stories are set. This corresponds approximately to Dorset, Somerset, Hampshire, and Wiltshire.

### RESEARCH ACTIVITIES

1 Look at a map of Wessex and a current map of the same area with details of towns and villages. Locate the following modern names. Hardy's names are in brackets:

   ◆ Dorchester (Casterbridge)
   ◆ Lulworth Cove (Lulwind Cove)
   ◆ Toller Down (Norcombe Hill)
   ◆ Puddletown (Weatherbury)
   ◆ Weymouth (Budmouth)
   ◆ Woodbury Hill nr Bere Regis (Greenhill)

2 Draw a map which shows the locations in the novel.

The WESSEX of Thomas Hardy's Novels & Poems

The setting of the novel is rural and 'outdoors'. The novel is a 'pastoral romance', and a number of important scenes happen outdoors – for example the hay-rick fire episode, which brings Oak back into Bathsheba's life, the sword exercise with Troy, and the Sheep Fair at Greenhill.

But there are also important 'interior' scenes. Oak nearly suffocating is one important interior; Troy waiting in the church for Fanny is another; and Boldwood's shooting of Troy is a third.

### WRITING ACTIVITIES

1 Re-read the episodes mentioned above and note the importance of the particular setting.
2 Find three or four other important interior and exterior episodes in the novel, in which the setting is significant. Make notes about this significance.

## PLOT

The word 'pastoral' as used above indicates a rural, country setting. The word 'romance' indicates relationships concerned with love. The plot of *Far From the Madding Crowd* can be analysed and divided into phases, in accordance with Bathsheba's relationships with three men: Oak, Boldwood, and Troy. See the Plot Table below.

| Chapters | Main narrative events |
|---|---|
| **1 to 11**<br>Key chapters:<br><br>4. Gabriel's Resolve<br><br>6. The Fair – The Journey – The Fire | Gabriel Oak, of Norcombe Hill, described as a sound, good character, meets the vain and attractive Bathsheba Everdene, new to the area. Oak soon proposes marriage, which she refuses. She then moves away to take tenancy of her late uncle's farm at Weatherbury. Oak, a successful and aspiring sheep farmer, loses his flock in an accident and is rendered penniless. He moves away to find work and happens upon a hay-rick fire, which he extinguishes. The grateful owner, who turns out to be Bathsheba, hires him. Oak encounters a frail Fanny Robin, who has run away from the Everdene farm to meet with Sgt Frank Troy, who says he will marry her. Meanwhile, Bathsheba sacks her bailiff for stealing and decides to run the farm herself. |
| **12 to 23**<br>Key chapters:<br><br>14. Effect of the Letter<br><br>19. The Sheep Washing – The Offer | Gentleman Farmer Boldwood calls on his new neighbour to enquire after the missing Fanny, but Bathsheba cannot meet him. Next day she is the centre of attention at the corn market where she makes a great impression on all except Boldwood. Bathsheba, capriciously and by chance, sends Boldwood a Valentine – which deeply moves and quickly obsesses him. Meanwhile, Fanny has tragically gone to the wrong church for her wedding to the now humiliated and furious Troy. Eventually Boldwood, having brooded, proposes marriage to Bathsheba, which she declines without absolutely refusing. Oak is asked his views on her liaison with Boldwood and is dismissed for bluntly expressing them. She begs and gains his return to save her flock of dying sheep. Boldwood seems favoured at the shearing supper and proposes to Bathsheba again. She replies that she hopes to be able to accept him when he returns from his planned journey. |
| **24 to 38**<br>Key chapter:<br>28. The Hollow Amid the Ferns | |
| **39 to 48**<br>Key chapters:<br><br>43. Fanny's Revenge<br><br>48. Doubts Arise – Doubts Linger | Troy, seeing Fanny again by chance, arranges to meet her at Casterbridge where, seeking refuge at the Workhouse, she dies that same night, in childbirth. Her coffin is brought back to Weatherbury, but, by chance, has to be kept at Bathsheba's house for the night. Bathsheba, suspicious and distraught at Troy's behaviour, opens Fanny's coffin, finding the dead child with her. Troy now returns and there takes place a harsh exchange of words between them. Bathsheba, mortified with grief at the full truth of her mistaken marriage, rushes out. Troy buries Fanny and plants her grave with flowers which are washed away in a downpour. He leaves Weatherbury and, while swimming, is swept out to sea by a strong current. A passing boat saves him but there is strong evidence that he is drowned. That Troy is dead is widely believed; a belief not wholly shared by Bathsheba. |
| **49 to 57**<br>Key chapter:<br>49. Oak's Advancement | |

## WRITING ACTIVITIES

**3** Copy the Plot Table and complete it for the two phases of the plot left blank, then select a second key chapter for each section.

**4** Read the ten key chapters now identified in the table as a revision exercise, noting their usefulness not only as key points in the story, but what they contribute on character and theme.

**5** When you have decided which chapters to focus on for revision and from which to select quotes, highlight the relevant sentence in the table. You can then see how it fits the narrative development.

## ESSAY QUESTIONS: SETTING AND PLOT

**1** Which episodes from the plot of *Far From the Madding Crowd* depend particularly upon their setting in order to engage and sustain the reader's interest? How does Hardy achieve the desired effect in those episodes?

**2** Explain what you understand by the term 'pastoral romance'. Explain how Hardy has achieved this in the novel with some close reference to setting and narrative development.

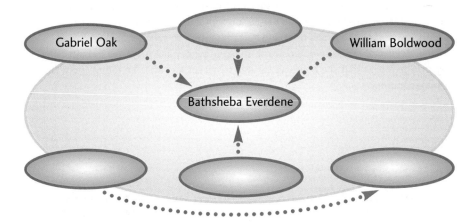

# CHARACTERS

The function of the character map is to put a picture in your mind, not only of the characters, but of their relationships. There are five major characters in the novel:

♦ Gabriel Oak
♦ Bathsheba Everdene
♦ William Boldwood
♦ Sgt Frank Troy
♦ Fanny Robin;

and two further sets of characters:

♦ Bathsheba's female workers
♦ the male workers on the farm and other locals.

## ▌WRITING ACTIVITIES

1 Copy and complete the seven boxes on the character map. Think about the best place to put each name.
2 Now connect the boxes and write along the lines the relationship between the characters or some basic fact of interest between them.
   **NB** They relate to each other as well as to Bathsheba.

## CHARACTER TRACKING

You will need to track the characters as you read through the novel, collecting key words and references for quotations as you go. These should be collected into a table for ease of remembering and revision.

| Character | Physical description | Who/what is he? Personality/ideas | Relationships |
| --- | --- | --- | --- |
| Gabriel Oak | Oak's wide smile is our first view of him so that his young face wrinkles 'like the rays . . . of the rising sun'. His usual dress is a low-crowned felt hat, a long coat with huge pockets, leather leggings, and boots. He is comfortable in his various working clothes but not in his Sunday suit. His large fob watch is mentioned in detail. His height and breadth are 'imposing' causing in him 'a faintly perceptible bend'. He is 28 in Chapter 1. Oak looks strong and has a solid figure. His surname is a metaphor for his physical appearance as well as his character. Physiognomy works well for Oak. | As the book opens, Oak is trying to establish independence as a sheep farmer. Later he is Bathsheba's shepherd, then bailiff, then overseer of two estates. Oak's character is established in the first few chapters and remains consistent throughout. He is: <br>◆ a man of good character <br>◆ steadfast and durable <br>◆ unselfish <br>◆ a guardian angel <br>◆ parochial rather than worldly <br>◆ usually calm and dignified <br>◆ reliable, realistic, and reflective <br>◆ a very good shepherd/farmer <br>◆ knowledgeable of country ways, seasons, the stars, the ways of folklore <br>◆ rational, 'indifferent to fate' <br>◆ a caring person (the encounter with Fanny shows this) – he also cares for his lambs <br>◆ courageous, persevering <br>◆ morally decenct <br>◆ perceptive of character and motives; he sees Bathsheba's vanity and capricious selfishness, Boldwood's suffering, and Troy's wasteful unscrupulousness. <br>He is also: <br>◆ tactless, outspoken, and brutally honest with Bathsheba <br>◆ sometimes stubborn <br>◆ lacking in romance. | Oak shows patient devotion towards Bathsheba throughout the book. Chapter 4 shows his naïve inability to win Bathsheba. Fate and circumstance, her frivolity, his steadfast care of her farming affairs, and his attempts to sanction and guide her, form their relationship for most of the book. Oak shows concern, sympathy, and generosity towards Boldwood, with whom he identifies as a sufferer in life – particularly after Troy appears. Oak shows concern and understanding towards Fanny in their brief meeting. Oak is clear about Troy's pernicious nature; he sees him as selfish, superficial, and destructive. They have little to do with each other in the novel. |

## WRITING ACTIVITIES

3 Look up the word 'physiognomy'; explain how the concept fits Oak and Troy.

4 In pairs, choose some of the descriptions, key words, and references to relationships in the table on the previous page and locate evidence from the text to support them.

5 Look for passages of dialogue between Oak and others. Comment on his use of language; how would you describe his speech patterns and vocabulary compared to those of Boldwood or Troy?

## ESSAY QUESTIONS: GABRIEL OAK

1 Fate and chance work against Oak and also for him, yet he seems oblivious to this. Explore this idea with reference to the first part of the book.

2 In Chapter 29, Hardy speaks of him as 'homely Oak, whose defects were patent to the blindest, and whose virtues were as metals in a mine'. Show that this description of Oak is supported by his actions, words, and personality.

| Character | Physical description | Who/what is she? Personality/ideas | Relationships |
|---|---|---|---|
| Bathsheba Everdene | Some physical descriptions of Bathsheba include: ◆ a handsome girl ◆ fair product of nature (Chapter 1) ◆ black hair ◆ correct facial curves (Chapter 17) ◆ keenly pointed corners of her red mouth ◆ exact arch of upper teeth ◆ lithe slip of humanity (Chapter 12) ◆ a woman in full bloom and vigour ◆ 'her new riding habit of myrtle green which fitted her to the waist as a rind fits its fruit' (Chapter 22) | ◆ vain ◆ capricious ◆ impulsive ◆ unconventional ◆ determined ◆ strong character ◆ desires romance ◆ complex nature ◆ vulnerable ◆ distressed ◆ remorseful ◆ cheerless | Bathsheba seems unable to comprehend the effect of her actions. In Chapter 19 her inability or disinclination to refuse Boldwood is a weakness, if not a serious flaw. This is compounded in Chapter 23 when she gives him greater hope. Hardy says that she is culpable (blameworthy) because of her inability to 'control feeling by subtle and careful enquiry into consequences' (Chapter 29). She becomes genuinely sorry for the Valentine prank. She suffers over Troy, as Boldwood suffers over her: ● Troy does not love her though she does love him ● Troy does love Fanny and regards her as his wife, even in death ● He treats herself, her farm, and her money with selfish contempt. |

## WRITING ACTIVITY

6 Look at the second column of the table above.

◆ Add key words according to your understanding, notes, and research on Bathsheba.

◆ What do you think are the most typical or dominant aspects of her character? How do these affect her relationships in different parts of the novel?

1 Track the events of the second phase of the novel, with a focus on Bathsheba's conversations with Boldwood and his deepening obsession. Do you think Bathsheba treats Boldwood badly?

2 Write an essay which explains Bathsheba's actions with Troy. You should include:
   ◆ her age and personality
   ◆ Troy's seductive persuasiveness
   ◆ references to the notion of romantic love
   ◆ considerations of the moral points Hardy might be presenting.

## OTHER MAJOR CHARACTERS

### WRITING ACTIVITY

In pairs or groups, divide the task of compiling character tables, as for Oak and Bathsheba above. Note references in the text which support your findings. Focus on the most relevant phases and chapters for detail.

### ESSAY QUESTIONS: OTHER MAJOR CHARACTERS

1 Is Boldwood a tragic character?

2 Compare the physical and personality attributes of Boldwood and Troy. Is Bathsheba's rejection of one and infatuation with the other understandable?

3 What is Fanny Robin's function in the novel? Is her plight a believable one, or does she simply serve a narrative and moral purpose for the author?

# NARRATIVE STRUCTURE

## SERIALIZATION

Hardy submitted the first few chapters of the novel for publication in *The Cornhill Magazine* in September 1873. The first episode appeared in January 1874 and there were twelve episodes, one per month throughout 1874. Serialization was a common form of publication for the Victorian novel. The author had to keep his or her audience interested, wanting to buy the next issue to find out what happens next. The novel was published as a whole in November 1874, just after Hardy and Emma Gifford returned from their honeymoon.

### WRITING ACTIVITIES

1 Look at the contents page and chapter headings of the novel.
   ◆ Divide the novel into twelve instalments, which may not be of equal length – remember that you need to end each instalment with a 'cliff-hanger'.

> ◆ Imagine you are an illustrator, and decide which episode you would illustrate, and why, for each instalment.
>
> **2** Look up the following website; it shows the 12 instalments and Helen Paterson's original illustrations. Compare it with your work for question 1 above.
> http://www.st-and.ac.uk/~ttha/illustrations/ffmc/cornhill/0.htm

## BATHSHEBA'S MEN

The most obvious structure in the book is its organization around Bathsheba Everdene and her relationships with three men.

> ### ▍WRITING ACTIVITY
>
> **3** Remind yourself of the chapters which relate to Bathsheba's attachments to Oak, Boldwood, and Troy. Devise a 'structure map', like the character map, to illustrate this. Add the following information to the map:
> ◆ major episodes in the relationships
> ◆ where the story of Fanny Robin fits in
> ◆ some comments on the change and development of Bathsheba's character as the novel progresses.

## THE SEASONS AND THE FARMING YEAR

A major structural feature of the novel is the farming year. Chapter 2 of the novel opens on 'the eve of St Thomas's, the shortest day of the year', that is, 21 December. The novel ends with the limited revival of Bathsheba's spirits in the spring following the shooting.

| Time | Event |
| --- | --- |
| **First year:** | |
| December–February | Lambing, Valentine's Day |
| March–May | Sheep washing |
| June | Sheep shearing, meeting Troy |
| Midsummer | Around 24 June, the sword exercise |
| August | Chapter 33, 'Lammas' time; on the 17th Troy marries Bathsheba |
| October–winter | Meeting Fanny; Fanny dies; Troy disappears; Bathsheba (almost) accepts his death |
| **Second year:** | |
| Winter–spring | Oak's advancement |
| Summer | Boldwood's renewed interest |
| Autumn | Greenhill Sheep Fair |
| December | Boldwood's Christmas Eve party |
| **Third year:** | |
| March | Boldwood's trial and reprieve |
| Spring | Oak and Bathsheba marry |

## WRITING ACTIVITY

**4** How do some of the major events in the novel relate to the time of year in which they take place? Comment on some of the links made in the table above.

## NIGHT AND DAY — LIGHT AND DARK

Another interesting structural aspect of the novel is Hardy's symbolic use of light and dark at various points, to reinforce mood or portend events to come.

- It is night-time when Gabriel loses his flock of sheep (Chapter 5).
- It is night-time when we meet Fanny outside Troy's barracks (Chapter 11).
- It is 'eventide' when Boldwood makes his second declaration to Bathsheba, which she seems to receive well (Chapter 23).
- It is the same night when she becomes entangled with Troy (Chapter 24).
- It is a bright evening when Troy does his romantic, symbolically sexual, sword exercise.

## WRITING ACTIVITY

**5** Choose a number of chapters at random. Identify whether they are set at night or in the daytime, and comment upon whether this is significant. You may include some of the examples above.

### ESSAY QUESTION: NARRATIVE STRUCTURE

Discuss the way Hardy structured his novel, with close reference to the text. How do these structures add to the reader's enjoyment of the book?

# THEMES

Hardy is concerned with three main themes. The novel is a pastoral romance and so elements of each genre will be the author's concern. Furthermore, there are numerous examples of chance and fate in the story – with both good and ill results – so these elements constitute a theme.

The novel touches upon other issues also:
- social conditions with regard to tenancy, employment, Poor Laws
- the situation of women, with Bathsheba pushing forward her boundaries, the working women reinforcing theirs, and Fanny as the helpless victim of a man and a social system
- isolation and despair, which also touch the main characters at some point in the novel.

The main themes, however, are these:

| | |
|---|---|
| **Love** | Love is represented in a number of guises in the novel, as portrayed in the main characters: <br> Oak – constant, patient, quiet, devoted, protective, companionable <br> Boldwood – obsessive, possessive, idealized, sexually repressed, violent, destructive <br> Troy – sexual, exciting, selfish, corrupting, unscrupulous, compelling <br> Bathsheba – vain, self-loving, flirtatious, impulsive, capricious; then mature, companionable, dependent <br> Fanny – naïve, forlorn, doomed, tragic. <br> The theme of love is treated in the novel in a circular way – corresponding to the circularity of the seasons. Oak, in Chapter 4, with his 'whenever you look up' speech, makes 'The Mistake'. Fifty-three chapters later, and after a lot of heartache all round, he achieves what he wants. |
| **The natural world** <br> Rural life | Rural life and the business of the farming community and its world are thematic in all of Hardy's Wessex novels. In this novel there are numerous references which are more than just a colourful backdrop to events – they are essential to the novel's meaning. These include: <br> ◆ the hiring fair <br> ◆ the organization of the farm, its men, its jobs <br> ◆ sheep washing, sheep shearing, the traditional supper <br> ◆ hay making and harvesting <br> ◆ bee-hiving <br> ◆ the sheep fair and entertainment <br> ◆ the village, the church, and the pub. |
| **The power of nature/the pathetic fallacy** | 'Pathetic fallacy' means the juxtaposition of the weather – snow, rain, storms, and cold – with events which their discomfort appears to reflect. A good example is the violent rush of torrential rainwater from the gargoyle which washes away the flowers on Fanny's grave. <br> Fire is also important in the novel, both fires in the hearth and accidental fires.  |
| **The universe/ time/knowledge** | Oak reads the stars and their positions, can foretell the weather, and is in tune with nature. In a pre-technological world, Oak's knowledge and skills are held in awe. |
| **Fate and chance** | It is Boldwood's personality and psychological make-up which determines his fate. But this is unleashed by the receipt of the Valentine, which was a matter of whimsical chance. <br> Troy is fated, too, by his psychological make-up. His pride causes him to reject Fanny after the fiasco of the wrong church, and his pursuit of beauty and wealth determines his ultimate exile and death. <br> In Chapter 6, Hardy speaks of Gabriel's 'indifference to fate', though fate has just dealt him a severe blow. <br> All of the main characters, to different extents, are the victims or beneficiaries of fate, chance, coincidence, or luck. |

## WRITING ACTIVITY

The following website is very useful and interesting – you can word-search the novel:

http://www.concordance.com/

Access the site and follow the instructions. Use the key words 'fate' and 'chance'. You will find eight occurrences of 'fate' and 16 of 'chance'. You can also access the surrounding text. Study these occurrences of the key words. What do they tell you of the importance of 'fate' and 'chance' in the novel?

## ESSAY QUESTIONS: THEMES

1 Discuss the ways that Hardy treats the theme of love, and how he shows us that patient, virtuous love will ultimately be rewarded and the excesses of desire, flirtatiousness and self-love will result in tragedy.

2 The novel may be called a 'pastoral romance'. What is 'pastoral' about it at its best, and how does Hardy's innate understanding of a rural community add to the reader's pleasure?

3 Henry James reputedly said, 'The only believable characters in *Far From the Madding Crowd* are the animals'. Is it at all fair to say that so much in the novel depends on fate, chance, and coincidence that most of the narrative development and many of the characters' actions are unbelievable?

## EXAMINATION QUESTIONS

1 Read again the passage from the end of Chapter 13, 'The Valentine', which concludes with Bathsheba sending the Valentine to Boldwood. How does the event affect Boldwood's life and character?

2 Read again the passage from the end of Chapter 40, 'On Casterbridge Highway', in which Fanny Robin finally reaches the Union. Would you agree that Fanny Robin is the character who suffers most in the novel?

3 How far can you understand and sympathize with Gabriel Oak throughout the novel? You should refer closely to his speech and actions.

4 What is the difference between Bathsheba in Chapter 54 and Bathsheba at the beginning of the novel? You should refer closely to events in your answer.

5 During the writing of this book, Hardy married his wife, Emma. To what extent can the novel be seen as a moral statement on marriage?

6 Consider the idea that the novel is about communication and isolation. In your answer you might include:

◆ an exploration of the times when the main characters are physically or mentally alone – or both

◆ the effect of this upon their actions and attitudes, and how these differ

◆ an examination of the misunderstandings which occur in the novel between Bathsheba and Oak, and Bathsheba and Boldwood.

# PRIDE AND PREJUDICE

## Jane Austen

> *Before beginning this unit, go back to pages 83–84 and read again what examiners are looking for in an essay about pre-1914 prose.*

## BACKGROUND AND CONTEXT

Jane Austen was born in 1775 at Steventon, Hampshire, where her father was rector. There were eight children in the family, and she was the seventh. Her closest companion was her only sister Cassandra, who was older. The children were tutored in Oxford and then went to Abbey School, Reading, until 1787, after which they were taught at home. Jane Austen's father was a scholar and her mother an intelligent and witty woman. The Austens were upper-middle-class gentry, a lively and affectionate family who enjoyed learning, literature, and the arts. She had a wide network of friends and relations in the village, the neighbourhood, London, and Bath. There was no shortage of characters, settings, and subject matter for her novels. There were a number of romantic attachments in Jane's life and it seems likely that once she agreed to marry, but changed her mind. Her sister later destroyed or censored Jane's letters, so the picture of her romantic attachments is vague.

Jane Austen probably began writing at the age of twelve. In her teenage years she wrote stories full of amusing fantasy, and a spoof 'History of England'. In her short lifetime she wrote seven novels and some unfinished work. When Jane was twenty-six the family moved to Bath, the setting for much of her writing. Five years later, on the death of her father, she moved with her sister and mother to Chawton in Hampshire. Here Jane wrote in earnest. She published *Sense and*

Sensibility in 1811, *Pride and Prejudice* in 1813, *Mansfield Park* in 1814 and *Emma* in 1815. These novels were successful and acclaimed, though their author remained anonymous. Her brother Henry arranged for *Persuasion* and *Northanger Abbey* to be published after her death in 1817, together with a biographical note. This was the first time the public knew her name or anything about her.

## RESEARCH ACTIVITIES

1 Find a time-line for Jane Austen which shows the movements in her life and the places which were important to her. Use a search engine of your choice, or browse the following website:
http://www.pemberley.com/janeinfo/janelife.html

2 Look at pictures of Jane and her family. What do the pictures tell you about their social class?

3 Read the extract below taken from a letter Jane wrote to Cassandra in 1796. What aspects of this letter remind you of the style and content of Jane Austen's fictional writing? Read some more of Jane Austen's letters on the following website: http://www.pemberley.com/janeinfo/janeinfo.html#janetoc

*Steventon: Thursday (January 16)*

*I have just received yours and Mary's letter, and I thank you both, though their contents might have been more agreeable. I do not at all expect to see you on Tuesday, since matters have fallen out so pleasantly; and if you are not able to return till after that day, it will hardly be possible for us to send for you before Saturday, though for my own part I care so little about the ball that it would be no sacrifice to me to give it up for the sake of seeing you two days earlier. We are extremely sorry for poor Eliza's illness. I trust, however, that she has continued to recover since you wrote, and that you will none of you be the worse for your attendance on her. What a good-for-nothing fellow Charles is to bespeak the stockings! I hope he will be too hot all the rest of his life for it!*

Jane Austen lived her life in a period of great turbulence in the world. The following are some major world events and their dates:

| Date | Event |
| --- | --- |
| 1783 | American independence |
| 1789 | French Revolution |
| 1793 | France declares war on Britain |
| 1800–1815 | Napoleon's campaigns in Europe and against Britain. |

**RESEARCH ACTIVITIES**

4 Using an encyclopaedia or history book, find some basic details about each of the events mentioned in the table.

5 The action of *Pride and Prejudice* takes place between September 1811 and just before Christmas 1812, when the double wedding is celebrated. Track the months and events as you re-read the novel. Note national events at the same key times.

For nearly all of the span of Jane Austen's life, Britain was at war, usually with France. Soldiers and the navy were an important and very obvious aspect of life. Young men were conscripted into the militia, or press-ganged into the navy, and there was a large regular army. The class from which Jane and her family came provided officers for the army and navy.

*Pride and Prejudice* is not directly touched by world events – the concerns of the novel are not the concerns of a country at war. Nor is Jane Austen concerned with social issues such as poverty or everyday working life. Great changes were happening to the country: the industrial revolution had taken hold, moving people from the countryside to the factories, especially in the north of England, where steam-powered machinery was producing wealth for a few and drudgery for the many. But this was not Jane Austen's world and is not the world of Elizabeth Bennet and her sisters. The Bennet family is concerned with keeping its position in society and establishing secure homes for the girls in the only way it can – through marriage; so the emphasis is on romance, balls, and eligible young men.

## MONEY

Money is important in *Pride and Prejudice*; directly or indirectly, it occupies the thoughts of Mrs Bennet for much of the time. We usually know how much bachelors are worth in Jane Austen's novels.

## ▌WRITING ACTIVITIES

**1** What do we know about the following financial matters:

- ◆ Darcy's income
- ◆ Darcy's capital wealth
- ◆ Bingley's wealth
- ◆ Mrs Bennet's expected income if Mr Bennet dies
- ◆ what Lydia costs her father per year?

**2** Read the beginning of Chapter 7 and of Chapter 13. What does the term 'entail' mean? Why is it important to the novel?

# CHARACTERS, RELATIONSHIPS, AND VIEWPOINTS

Study the family trees below and fix all of the characters and their interactions in your mind.

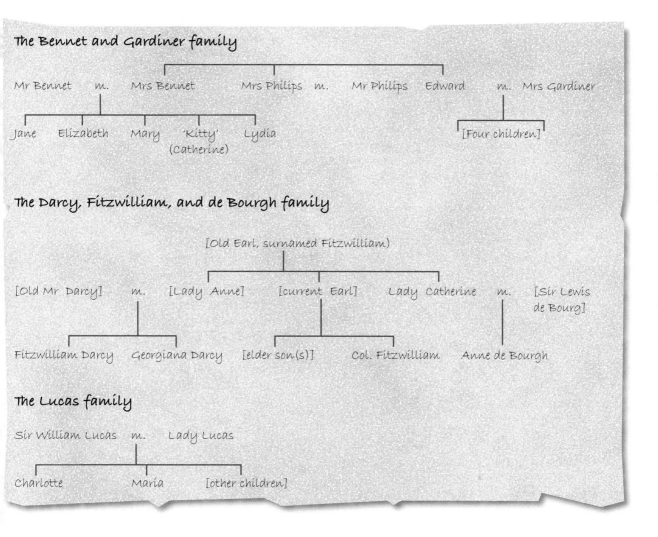

### The Bennet and Gardiner family

Mr Bennet  m.  Mrs Bennet    Mrs Philips  m.  Mr Philips    Edward  m.  Mrs Gardiner

Jane  Elizabeth  Mary  'Kitty'  Lydia          [Four children]
                        (Catherine)

### The Darcy, Fitzwilliam, and de Bourgh family

[Old Earl, surnamed Fitzwilliam)

[Old Mr Darcy]  m.  [Lady Anne]    [current Earl]    Lady Catherine  m.  [Sir Lewis de Bourg]

Fitzwilliam Darcy  Georgiana Darcy    [elder son(s)]  Col. Fitzwilliam    Anne de Bourgh

### The Lucas family

Sir William Lucas  m.  Lady Lucas

Charlotte    Maria    [other children]

| Character | Who/what is he/she? | Personality | Viewpoint, relationships | References |
|---|---|---|---|---|
| Mr Bennet | Owner of Longbourn House in Hertfordshire. The estate earns him £2,000 a year. He has been married to Mrs Bennet for 23 years. | Mr Bennet is 'a mixture of quick parts, sarcastic humour, reserve, and caprice'. He is witty and clever. Elizabeth shares some of his characteristics and she is his favourite. He is 'fond of the country and of books; and from these tastes had arisen his principal enjoyments'. This compensates for a marriage which gives him no joy. | Mr Bennet withdraws to his library and makes little contribution to family matters or his wife's interests. The notable exception is his 'interview' with Elizabeth about marrying Mr Collins. Elizabeth is aware of the 'impropriety of her father's behaviour as a husband'. She feels he could have done more to save his wife and younger daughters from their own stupidity and frivolity. | Ch 1<br><br>Beginning of Ch 7 (p 75)<br><br>Beginning of Ch 42 (p 262)<br><br>Middle of Ch 20 (p 152)<br><br>Middle of Ch 39 (p 248) |
| Mrs Bennet | The husband of the above and mother of five daughters. Daughter of Meryton attorney. Inherited £4,000 which gives her a small independent income. Mr Bennet was 'captivated by youth and beauty, and that appearance of good humour' which she had at the presumably young age he first met her. | Mrs Bennet 'was a woman of mean understanding, little information, and uncertain temper. When she was discontented, she fancied herself nervous.' She is insensitive, embarrassingly crass, self-centred, prejudiced, gossiping, loud, and lacks decorum. She also lacks sound judgement and reason. | She shows misguided pride and is prejudiced against most people at one time or another. The great irony of her viewpoint is that, although 'The business of her life was to get her daughters married', her lack of decorum and thoughtlessness make it more difficult for Elizabeth and Jane to make suitable marriages. 'People who suffer as I do from nervous complaints can have no great inclination for talking. Nobody can tell what I suffer! – But it is always so. Those who do not complain are never pitied.' The irony here is that she constantly talks, and always complains. | Mrs Bennet is more evident throughout the novel than her husband.<br><br>Ch 1<br><br>Beginning of Ch 7 (p 75)<br><br>End of Ch 18 (pp 144–5)<br><br>Ch 20<br><br>Beginning of Ch 23 (pp 167–8)<br><br>Beginning of Ch 25 (pp 177–8)<br><br>Beginning of Ch 42 (p 262) |

## WRITING ACTIVITIES

1 Read the first page of Chapter 42, where we see aspects of Mr Bennet's character through Elizabeth's eyes. What does this tell us of the man's outlook and personality? Collect key words and brief quotations for these two characters.

2 Read the beginning of Chapter 23, where Mrs Bennet is informed that Charlotte Lucas is to marry Mr Collins. What does her behaviour as reported tell us of her character?

| Character | Who/what is she? | Personality | Viewpoint, relationships | References |
|---|---|---|---|---|
| Elizabeth | The second eldest Bennet daughter, aged 20 and the heroine of the novel. Her father's favourite, though her mother considers her 'not a bit better than the others', 'not half so handsome as Jane nor half so good humoured as Lydia'. Sometimes called Lizzie or Eliza. | Elizabeth is intelligent, lively, quick-witted. She is perceptive and sensitive – particularly to her mother's failings. She is sensible but not staid. She is capable of affection, love, and strong feeling, but always within reason and with appropriate behaviour. 'She had a lively, playful disposition, which delighted in any thing ridiculous.' She has strength of character and self-belief. | It is largely from Elizabeth's viewpoint that events and people are viewed. She misjudges Wickham and Darcy. Her pride is flattered by Wickham. Her prejudice blinds her to Darcy's character. Her view of Darcy is wrong; she misjudges his intentions and honesty. She realizes her mistakes and regrets them, feeling she has lost a great chance for happiness. Her viewpoint (and Darcy's) develops through the novel in an important way. | Ch 3, the ball at Meryton<br><br>Ch 16, Elizabeth meets and is impressed by Wickham<br><br>Chs 19 and 20, Collins's proposal and Elizabeth's reaction<br><br>Chs 31–34, meetings between Elizabeth and Darcy<br><br>Ch 34, Darcy's proposal<br><br>Ch 35, Darcy's letter<br><br>Chs 36–37, Elizabeth's regret and realization |
| Jane | At 22, the eldest daughter, often referred to as Miss Bennet in the novel. Close to Elizabeth. Eventually marries Bingley. | Considered the prettiest of the daughters. Bingley sees her at the Meryton ball, 'and as to Miss Bennet, he could not conceive an angel more beautiful'. *Using some of the references in the right-hand column, list some more key words and phrases to describe Jane's personality.* | Lacks pride or prejudice. In Chapter 4, Lizzie says of her sister, 'Oh! you are a great deal too apt, you know, to like people in general.' *In Chapter 17 Jane speaks well of both Darcy and Wickham. What does she say which illuminates her view of life and people? Does Jane's view of Lydia's elopement (Chapter 46) verge on naïve stupidity? Explain.* | Ch 4, Lizzie on Jane<br><br>Beginning of Ch 17, Jane on Darcy and Wickham<br><br>Ch 21, Jane on Caroline Bingley<br><br>Ch 24, Jane's disappointment<br><br>Ch 26 (pp184–5), Jane's letter about Miss Bingley<br><br>Ch 46, Jane's letters about Lydia |

## WRITING ACTIVITIES

**3** In pairs, choose some of the words and phrases used above to describe Elizabeth's personality, and locate evidence from the text to support them.

**4** Read Chapter 3 and study the description of Darcy and Elizabeth at the Meryton ball. Explain what is significant about this episode.

**5** Elizabeth reads Darcy's letter (Chapter 35) 'with a strong prejudice against everything he might say' but with an 'eagerness which hardly left her power of comprehension' (Chapter 36). Why and how is this letter the turning point of the novel?

**6** It may be said that Jane completely lacks either pride or prejudice. Respond to this suggestion with reference to the questions in the table above.

| Character | Who/what is he/she? | Personality | Viewpoint, relationships |
|---|---|---|---|
| Darcy | Son of Mr Darcy the elder, who died approximately five years before the novel begins, and Lady Anne Fitzwilliam (sister to Lady Catherine de Bourgh). Lives at Pemberley in Derbyshire and has a town house in London. 28 years old, with an income of £10,000. | He is described as a 'fine, tall person, handsome features, noble mien'. He has an aristocratic bearing and persona. He seems to be haughty and proud, unable to suffer fools gladly and Mrs Bennet not at all. His tendency to appear arrogant and snobbish is developed for the reader through Elizabeth's prejudice against him. His qualities of fairness, judiciousness, generosity, and responsibility – as well as his capacity to be mistaken – are all the more effectively and poignantly shown in contrast to Elizabeth's prejudice against him. | He snubs Elizabeth in Chapter 3 (p 59): 'She is tolerable; but not handsome enough to tempt *me*'. His viewpoint regarding Elizabeth changes gradually, as he recognizes the intelligence in her dark eyes (Chapter 6, p 70). He discusses aspects of his viewpoint with Elizabeth: 'My temper would perhaps be called resentful. My good opinion once lost is lost for ever' (Chapter 11, p 102). His anger and surprise at Elizabeth's rejection of his proposal is telling (Chapter 34, p 222). The letter he writes to Elizabeth is pivotal to an understanding of his character and viewpoint. It is the turning point in the novel (Chapter 35, p 226). |
| Lady Catherine de Bourgh | Sister of Darcy's mother. She is referred to as 'Lady' followed by her first name because she is the daughter of a higher nobleman. | Self-important, opinionated, thinks she is always right, rude and ill-mannered at times. | She is full of pride and prejudice: pride in her own lofty position, and prejudice against the possibility of Elizabeth marrying Darcy. In Chapter 56 she tries to get her own way by bullying Elizabeth – but fails. |

## WRITING ACTIVITIES

**7** Mr Darcy and Lady Catherine de Bourgh are related and it is her wish that he should marry her daughter. Comment upon the sort of people they seem to be.

**8** How does Elizabeth hold her own with Lady Catherine during their conversation in Chapter 56?

| Character | Who/what is he/she? | Personality | Viewpoint, relationships |
|---|---|---|---|
| William Collins | Rector of Hunsford in Kent. He attended Oxford or Cambridge university. He is 25. He is Mr Bennet's cousin. He will inherit the Longbourn estate. He marries Charlotte Lucas. | 'He was a tall, heavy looking young man of five and twenty. His air was grave and stately, and his manners were very formal' (Chapter 13, p 109). *What does Collins' manner in proposing to Elizabeth in Chapter 19 show us of his pomposity and his conceit?* 'My dear Jane, Mr Collins is a conceited, pompous, narrow-minded, silly man', says Elizabeth to Jane (Chapter 24, p 174). The letter to Mr Bennet about Lydia (Chapter 48) shows the selfish and unChristian side of his character. | Austen satirizes Collins greatly in the novel – which makes his character a source of considerable entertainment. His desire to marry a Bennet to keep the property in the family is not kind or romantic (Chapter 19, p 148). His viewpoint is: <br> ◆ materialistic <br> ◆ egocentric <br> ◆ proud <br> ◆ sycophantic towards Lady de Bourgh (beginning of Chapter 14, beginning of Chapter 29) <br> ◆ unChristian. |
| Charlotte Lucas | Eldest daughter of Sir William and Lady Lucas. Aged 27, and Elizabeth's best friend. | She is a sensible, intelligent woman. She is realistic and pragmatic. | She has a down-to-earth attitude to life and marriage, believing that happiness in marriage is 'entirely a matter of chance' (Chapter 6, p 69). <br><br> 'I am not romantic, you know. I never was. I ask only a comfortable home' (Chapter 22, p 165). |

### ▮ WRITING ACTIVITY

**9** In pairs, look carefully at the letter Collins writes to Mr Bennet in Chapter 48. List the ways in which Mr Collins manages to be offensive. Anthony Trollope called it 'a comic masterpiece'; what did he mean?

## STYLE AND THEME

*Pride and Prejudice*, like most of Jane Austen's novels, is a **comedy of manners**. It is a **comedy** because there is nothing in it which is tragic, nothing which evokes pity in the reader, nothing about deprivation, poverty, abuse, or hardship.

The **manners** explored in the novel are those of the middle and upper classes, obsessed with their world of romantic and financial intrigue, relationships, and squabbles.

Austen's novels are **classical** in style, which means that they conform to a certain structure and deal with a specific part of society. Very little actually happens in Jane Austen's novels – certainly not of a dramatic or extraordinary nature. In this novel, Lydia's elopement is the most shocking event that occurs.

It is Austen's **ironic** style which makes her novels engaging and enjoyable. Her **satire** of the manners and preoccupations of her characters shows the reader their weaknesses and, where there are any, their strengths.

There are numerous examples of ironic style in the novel; the letter to Mr Bennet from Collins is a good example. Collins presumably believes that his remarks are reasonable, helpful, consoling, compassionate, and supportive. They are, in fact, unChristian, offensive, self-serving, and ignorant. Collins' manners are thus exposed to the reader through Austen's language. The irony is that Collins does not see what we see; the gap between Collins' view of the letter and ours is comic.

The characteristics of the people in Austen's novels constitute some of the themes of the novel. For example, 'pomposity' is a theme, and the character of Mr Collins exemplifies it.

Other major themes are:
- pride
- prejudice
- love and marriage
- money.

### RESEARCH ACTIVITIES

1  Refer to the website www.concordance.com, which offers a word-search procedure for novels. You will find that there are 47 occurrences of the word 'pride' in the novel, six of 'prejudice', and 66 of 'marriage'. Track some of these, or search by character and theme to narrow down your analysis.

2  Refer to the website http://www.pemberley.com/janeinfo/janewrit.html#pridpreji for more on the novel and its themes.

## LANGUAGE

Austen's use of language is distinctive, and it is the key to enjoying and understanding her writing. She uses irony, wit, and complex sentences which reflect the social status of her characters.

There is no elaborate use of imagery in her writing. Her preoccupation is with people and their foibles, mannerisms, and attitudes. The novel contains no colloquialisms or dialect (unlike Hardy's, for example), and its formality reflects the eighteenth-century classicism of which it is a part.

The following extract is taken from Chapter 6, p 72, and is set 'at Sir William Lucas's where a large party were assembled'.

'My dear Miss Eliza, why are not you dancing? – Mr Darcy, <u>you must allow me to present</u> this young lady to you as a <u>very desirable partner</u>. – You cannot refuse to dance, I am sure, <u>when so much beauty is before you</u>.' And taking her hand, he would have given it to Mr Darcy, who, though extremely surprised, was not unwilling to receive it, when <u>she instantly drew back, and said with some discomposure to Sir William</u>,

'Indeed, Sir, I have not the least intention of dancing. – <u>I entreat you</u> not to suppose that I moved this way <u>in order to beg for a partner</u>.'

Mr Darcy with <u>grave propriety</u> requested to be allowed the honour of her hand; but in vain. Elizabeth was determined; <u>nor did Sir William at all shake her purpose</u> by his attempt at persuasion.

'<u>You excel so much in the dance, Miss Eliza</u>, that it is cruel to deny me the happiness of seeing you; and though <u>this gentleman dislikes the amusement in general, he can have no objection, I am sure, to oblige us for one half hour</u>.'

'<u>Mr Darcy is all politeness,' said Elizabeth, smiling</u>.

'He is indeed – <u>but considering the inducement, my dear Miss Eliza, we cannot wonder at his complaisance</u>; for who would object to such a partner?'

Elizabeth <u>looked archly</u>, and turned away. Her resistance had <u>not injured her with the gentleman</u>, and he was thinking of her with some <u>complacency</u>, when thus <u>accosted</u> by Miss Bingley.

## DISCUSSION ACTIVITY

Read the above extract carefully, focusing on the underlined phrases. Discuss with a partner how these words and phrases relate to the following aspects of Austen's writing style:

- formal politeness and propriety (proper manners)
- delicacy of expression and vocabulary
- feminine mannerism
- gentle irony
- powerful irony, verging on satire
- reference to feelings
- use of abstract nouns
- use of unusual/old-fashioned words.

## WRITING ACTIVITY

Mrs Bennet and Mr Collins are characters who give Austen the greatest scope for language full of ironic wit. Choose some examples to write about from the extracts noted for these characters in the tables above.

## EXAMINATION QUESTIONS

1  Which character do you think is Jane Austen's most interesting creation in the novel: Jane Bennet, Charlotte Lucas, or Lady Catherine de Bourgh? You should refer closely to all three characters; the language of their conversations, and some of the events which surround them in the novel.

2  In the following extract from Chapter 50, Elizabeth is reflecting on what might have been with Darcy:

> She was humbled, she was grieved; she repented, though she hardly knew of what. She became jealous of his esteem, when she could no longer hope to be benefited by it. She wanted to hear of him, when there seemed the least chance of gaining intelligence. She was convinced that she could have been happy with him, when it was no longer likely they should meet.
>
> What a triumph for him, as she often thought, could he know that the proposals which she had proudly spurned only four months ago, would now have been gladly and gratefully received! He was as generous, she doubted not, as the most generous of his sex. But while he was mortal, there must be a triumph.

Trace the relationship between Elizabeth and Darcy which has led Elizabeth to these thoughts. Austen's use of language should be considered in your answer.

# OF MICE AND MEN
## John Steinbeck

> *Before beginning this unit, go back to pages 83–84 and read again what examiners are looking for in an essay about post-1914 prose.*

## BACKGROUND AND CONTEXT

John Steinbeck was born in Salinas, California, in 1902, an area that he came to know very well during his boyhood explorations, and which he used as the setting for *Of Mice and Men*. He left university without completing the course and had a variety of jobs, including working on a ranch. He used this experience to help him when he wrote about the attitudes and lifestyle of the migrant workers in *Of Mice and Men*.

The novel was published in 1937, during the Great Depression which followed Wall Street Crash (the collapse of the New York Stock Exchange in 1929). During the 1930s many businesses failed, leading to huge numbers of unemployed. The only option for people who became very poor was to travel around looking for work. These migrant workers travelled alone and travelled light – they had very few belongings and rarely stayed in one place for long. Once a job was finished, they had to move on. However, many refused to give in to despair, and dreamed of eventually owning their own place and settling down. This 'American Dream' is shared by George and Lennie.

The title is taken from the poem *To a Mouse* by the Scottish poet Robert Burns. The seventh verse reads:

But Mousie, thou art no thy lane,    *[not alone]*
In proving foresight may be vain;
The best-laid schemes o' mice an' men
    Gang aft agley,    *[go often wrong]*
An' lea'e us nought but grief an' pain,
    For promised joy!

### ▮ DISCUSSION ACTIVITY

Consider the meaning of this verse and its relevance to the novel.

1 Investigate the following:
   - the Wall Street Crash   ◆ the Great Depression   ◆ Steinbeck's life.
2 How has Steinbeck used current events and personal experience in his novel?

# PLOT AND STRUCTURE

The events of the novel take place over a very few days – from Thursday evening to Sunday afternoon.

| | |
|---|---|
| Thursday evening | George and Lennie arrive at the clearing and camp for the night. |
| Friday 10 a.m. | George and Lennie arrive at the ranch. |
| Friday afternoon | George and Lennie work in the fields. |
| Friday evening | The evening is spent in the bunkhouse; Candy's old dog is shot, Lennie crushes Curley's hand. |
| Saturday evening | George goes with the others into Soledad. Lennie visits Crooks in his room; they are joined first by Candy and then by Curley's wife. |
| Sunday afternoon | The men play horseshoes while Lennie is in the barn with his dead puppy. He accidentally kills Curley's wife, and goes to hide in the clearing. George arrives and shoots Lennie. |

Some of these events are described in detail, as if they are happening 'on-stage' – in full view of the reader. Others happen 'off-stage' – they can be heard, but we do not see them. They do, however, intrude into the action 'on-stage'.

## WRITING ACTIVITIES

1 Create a chart showing the events that are described 'on-stage' under the headings when/who/where/what.
   Now produce a similar chart for events which happen 'off-stage'. For example: 'Friday evening, Carlson, outside the bunkhouse, shoots Candy's dog.'
2 Why do you think Steinbeck structured the novel in this way?
3 Is there any significant difference between incidents that occur 'off-stage' and those that are 'on-stage'?
4 What do the 'off-stage' incidents add to the atmosphere?

## PLOT SUMMARY

George and Lennie, two migrant workers, have left their last job in Weed in a hurry. They are on their way to a ranch near Soledad, but the bus driver dropped them off too soon. They find a small clearing near a pool and George decides they will stay there for the night.

During the course of the evening, George becomes cross with Lennie, firstly because he has a dead mouse in his pocket, then because Lennie complains that they have no ketchup. George then feels guilty and Lennie gets him to describe their dream of owning their own land. George says that he will do the talking when they arrive at the ranch – Lennie is big and strong and a good worker, but not very bright and George doesn't want them to lose the job because of this.

## WRITING ACTIVITIES

5 What mood is George in at the start of the novel? Can this be justified?

6 Why does Lennie keep the dead mouse? What does this tell us about him?

7 Why does George say their friendship is unique?

8 Explain their dream in your own words.

When they arrive at the ranch on Friday morning, they first meet Candy and his old crippled dog. The boss complains about their late arrival and is suspicious about why George does all the talking and why the two men travel together. His son Curley, an ex-boxer, takes an instant dislike to Lennie. Curley's wife later comes into the bunkhouse looking for her husband. Lennie is fascinated by her but George warns him that she could cause trouble.

The workers return for lunch. George and Lennie meet the leader Slim, whose team they join in the afternoon. Slim is impressed by Lennie's strength.

## WRITING ACTIVITIES

9 Why do you think George aggressively questions Candy about the state of the bunkhouse?

10 Why does George become angry with Lennie after the boss leaves?

11 What is it about Lennie that makes Curley dislike him?

12 Why does Lennie find Curley's wife so fascinating?

That evening, George talks to Slim about his friendship and explains why they had to leave Weed in such a hurry.

Carlson and Candy come in after playing horseshoes. Carlson complains about the smell of Candy's old dog and offers to put it out of its misery by shooting it. Slim, whose word appears to be law in the bunkhouse, agrees with Carlson and offers Candy one of his bitch's newly born puppies – Lennie clearly wants one too. Carlson takes the old dog out, and the atmosphere becomes heavy until they hear the shot.

Slim leaves the bunkhouse for a short time at the request of Crooks, the negro stable buck, and Curley bursts in looking for him, suspecting Slim to be with his wife. George and Whit play cards and agree that Curley's wife is troublesome. George and Lennie again talk of their dream for the future. Candy overhears and offers his savings if they will let him join them. The dream stands a chance of becoming reality.

Slim returns, followed by an apologetic Curley. Lennie does not notice this as he is still thinking about his dream and smiling to himself. Unfortunately, Curley needs to save face; he picks on Lennie and begins to punch him. Lennie is scared of George being angry with him and does not retaliate until George orders him to. Lennie completely crushes Curley's hand. Slim makes Curley promise not to say who injured him.

## WRITING ACTIVITIES

13 Why does Slim find George and Lennie's friendship so unusual?

14 In your own words, explain the circumstances surrounding George and Lennie's escape from Weed.

15 What does Curley's behaviour tell you about his personality and relationship with his wife?

16 What do you feel about the likelihood of the dream becoming a reality?

The following evening – Saturday – George goes with the other ranchers into Soledad, probably to have a drink at Susy's place. Lennie is left behind, as are Candy and Crooks.

Lennie is in the barn stroking his puppy, and seeing Crooks's light he goes up to his room and tries to make friends. At first, Crooks claims to be angry, but then he teases Lennie by saying George may not come back. Lennie cannot grasp this idea and becomes threatening. Candy appears just in time to calm things by talking about their plans for the future. Crooks cynically says they have no chance of realizing their dream – he has seen so many men dream and fail.

Curley's wife appears at the door – Lennie stares at her, and the other two go very quiet. She wants to know what happened to Curley's hand and works out that Lennie injured him. When Crooks asks her to leave, she becomes nasty and threatening. Candy gets her to leave by saying he has heard the men returning from town.

## ▌WRITING ACTIVITIES

17  What do you think of George leaving Lennie behind?

18  Why is Crooks so defensive at first? Why does he finally invite Lennie to sit down?

19  What does the description of Crooks's room tell you about him and his situation?

20  What are Crooks's views on loneliness?

21  What does Curley's wife threaten to do to Crooks? What is your opinion of this?

On Sunday afternoon, most of the men are outside the barn playing horseshoes. Lennie is again in the barn with his puppy, but it is dead because he has handled it too roughly. He is scared of George being angry and not letting him look after the rabbits.

Curley's wife comes into the barn. In response to Lennie talking about not being able to look after the rabbits, she talks about her failed ambition to become a film star. They agree that soft things are nice to touch and she invites Lennie to stroke her hair, but then, worried that he will mess it up, she asks him to stop. Lennie becomes scared and covers her mouth to keep her quiet. She panics and in the ensuing struggle, he breaks her neck. He realizes that he has done something very bad, and runs off to hide near the clearing where they spent Thursday night – as George had told him to do if there was any trouble.

The body of Curley's wife is found by Candy, who quietly fetches George. The others arrive, and set off to search for Lennie. George sends them in the wrong direction.

## ▌WRITING ACTIVITIES

22  Why does Curley's wife think she did not become a film star? Do you believe her?

23  Why does Lennie panic?

24  Why do you think Candy fetches George first?

25  Why does George ask Candy to wait a few minutes before raising the alarm?

26  Why does George send the men in the wrong direction?

Lennie arrives at the clearing as George had told him to. In his imagination, he hears his aunt Clara telling him off, followed by a giant rabbit that says George will leave him.

George arrives, but is not angry. He begins to talk about their dream, and encourages Lennie to look across the river. He then takes out Carlson's gun and shoots Lennie. The other men come in response to the gun shot, and assume that George shot Lennie in self-defence. Slim seems to understand. The dream will now never happen.

## WRITING ACTIVITIES

**27** Why do you think George is not angry? What emotion is he more likely to be feeling?

**28** Why does he kill Lennie rather than turning him in?

**29** Compare Lennie's death with that of Candy's old dog – what similarities are there? Why do you think this is?

### ESSAY QUESTION: PLOT AND STRUCTURE

To what extent do the speed and straightforwardness of the plot contribute to the novel's success?

# SETTING AND ATMOSPHERE

The novel has three main settings:

- the clearing             • the bunkhouse
- the barn – including Crooks's room.

The story starts and finishes in the clearing, making the novel cyclical.

Look again at the opening two paragraphs. Notice the following details:

- the river 'runs deep and green'
- the water 'has slipped twinkling over the yellow sands'
- 'the golden foothill slopes curve upwards'
- the willows are 'fresh and green'
- the sycamores have 'mottled, white, recumbent limbs'
- 'rabbits come out of the brush to sit on the sand'.

## WRITING ACTIVITY

**1** What atmosphere is created by these opening paragraphs?

Now look at the first three paragraphs of the last section, when Steinbeck describes the clearing before Lennie's return.

## WRITING ACTIVITY

**2** To what extent are the details of this setting similar? What is the effect of this?

Now go back to the beginning and remind yourself of the arrival of George and Lennie as 'the shade climbed up the hills' and 'the rabbits hurried noiselessly for cover'; 'a stilted heron laboured up into the air', and 'for a moment, the place was lifeless'. Then, later, as 'the tops of the Gabilan mountains flamed with the light of the sun', 'a water snake slipped along on the pool, its head held up like a periscope'.

Look for similarities in the last section, where 'the hilltops were rosy in the sun', 'a motionless heron . . . stood in the shallows', and a water snake was 'twisting its periscope head from side to side'. One difference on this occasion is that 'from out of Lennie's head came a gigantic rabbit'.

### WRITING ACTIVITY

**3** Consider the references to colour, light, movement, and sound, and comment on the mood and atmosphere that are created.

Now look at the change to the atmosphere in the clearing first when George and Lennie arrive, and later when Lennie returns on his own. Examine carefully Steinbeck's choice of words and images. Look for similarities and differences, and consider reasons for these as well as the effectiveness of Steinbeck's description.

The other settings are the bunkhouse, the barn, and Crooks's room. Look at the start of the second chapter of the novel, which begins with the description of the bunkhouse.

♦ What physical details are given?
♦ Which details concern colour, light, and sound?
♦ How effective is the description?
♦ Again, notice how the atmosphere is changed by the arrival of people.

Examine the beginning of each chapter, noticing how Steinbeck focuses on physical detail, sound, colour, and movement, before introducing people, action, and dialogue. Notice how each section begins with a descriptive passage. Chapter 4, for example, presents the reader with a detailed description of Crooks's room before Lennie blunders in; Chapter 5 opens in the barn, where the sound of the game of horseshoes intrudes upon Lennie's unhappiness.

Create a diagram for each section. For example, for Chapter 3 you could start as follows:

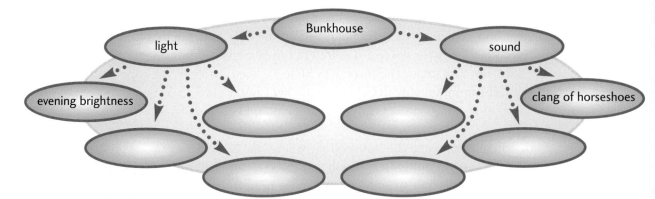

**WRITING ACTIVITY**

4  Make careful notes on the details of Steinbeck's descriptions of setting and
atmosphere.

**ESSAY QUESTION: SETTING AND ATMOSPHERE**

How do the various settings of the novel, and Steinbeck's creation of atmosphere,
add to the tension and tragedy of the novel?

## CHARACTERS

This section will help you to track the characters and prepare you for
essay questions on them.

One of the key aspects of Steinbeck's characters is contrast – contrast
between size, personality, colour, strength, etc.

The most obvious characters to start with are George and Lennie, as
they travel together and clearly rely on each other. Begin by looking at
the third paragraph of the novel. Initially, they appear to be alike
because what they are wearing, carrying, and doing are similar. Next
George is described, and then 'his opposite', Lennie.

**WRITING ACTIVITY**

1  Create a character map each for George and Lennie. Add details about the
features of appearance and personality that are presented in the first chapter. A
character map for George is started for you on the next page.

As you read through the novel, add to your notes/maps and keep a
note of key quotations to support what you find. You need to notice
what the characters say and do, and how other characters react to
them.

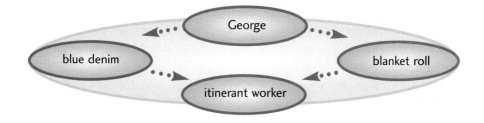

## GEORGE

The physical details about George that we are given at the start include 'small and quick', 'sharp, strong features', 'slender arms'. You can add to this list, and notice how some of these details are repeated later in the novel. What do they suggest about his personality?

George is the first to speak – and it is to give an order 'sharply' to Lennie. Notice how many orders George gives, and the words Steinbeck chooses to show how he talks to Lennie – words like 'angrily' and 'disgustedly'. What does this suggest about George's mood? What can you deduce about his attitude towards and relationship with Lennie? Notice how he seems to go from being angry to caring. Why do you think this is?

### ▌ WRITING ACTIVITY

> **2** Look closely at the way George is presented in the first chapter. What can you work out about him? Would you like him as a friend?

In Chapter 2, George is clearly the dominant one of the two. He seems to defend Lennie as well as get cross with him. Why do you think this is? Notice what George does in this chapter:

- He snaps at Candy – why? Is he just suspicious and bad tempered, or is he looking after himself and Lennie?
- He does not stay angry for long – notice when and why he changes his attitude. What does this add to your understanding of him?
- How does he behave when the boss appears? How do you explain this? Again, consider Steinbeck's choice of words and the different ways he behaves towards the boss and Lennie.
- How does George react when Curley appears? Notice words like 'coldly', 'tense'.
- Notice how soon Candy confides in George. How does George respond? What does this tell you about him?
- Now look at his reaction to Curley's wife, again finding key words and noting what you can deduce about George from this.

By the end of Chapter 2, you should have a clear picture of George and the way others respond to him. Continue to track his behaviour and relationships as you study the rest of the novel. Notice what he says and does, how he reacts to others – particularly Lennie – and how they react to him. For example, can you explain why Candy confides in George, and compare this with why George later confides in Slim?

As you track George through the novel, you might like to consider the following:

- Why does George stay with Lennie even though he is so much trouble? Is it just because of his promise to Aunt Clara or is there more to it than that?
- Why is he so suspicious about the bunks?
- Why does he get cross with Lennie for speaking to the boss?
- What does he confide to Slim, and why?
- Why does he tell Lennie about their dream so often?
- Why does he let Candy join them?
- Why does he encourage Lennie to fight back when attacked by Curley?
- Why does he go into town on Saturday night?
- Why does he shoot Lennie?

There are many more points to consider, but these will help you begin to understand George.

## LENNIE

You should also track Lennie throughout the novel, again noting what he says and how he says it, what he does, and how he responds to others. Is there any difference in the way he responds to George and to the others, for example?

Consider the following:

- Why does he copy George so closely?
- Why does he have a dead mouse in his pocket?
- Why does he lie about the mouse?
- Why does he complain about the lack of ketchup?
- How does he use George's guilt to his advantage?
- Why does he become so excited when George talks about their dream?
- Why is he so fascinated by Curley's wife?
- Why does he spend so much time with his puppy?
- Why does he not fight Curley until instructed to by George?
- Why is he not put off by Crooks's unwelcoming attitude?

- Why does he kill his puppy?
- Why does he kill Curley's wife?
- Why does he expect George to be angry with him?

As you keep track of characters, make sure you find suitable quotations to support what you say.

## ESSAY QUESTIONS: CHARACTERS

1 How do George and Lennie benefit from their friendship?
2 Why do you consider Candy and Slim to be important characters in the novel? You need to think about what they say and do as well as their relationship with other characters.

# THEMES AND ISSUES

## LONELINESS

This is perhaps the main theme of the novel. George and Lennie are different from the other workers because they do not travel alone. This is commented upon by others, who are suspicious of their friendship.

- The boss asks: 'What stake you got in this guy?'
- Curley demands: 'What the hell are you getting' into it for?'
- Slim comments: 'Funny how you an' him string along together.'

These details are in clear contrast to George's words in Chapter 1: 'Guys like us . . . are the loneliest guys in the world. They got no family. They don't belong no place . . . They ain't got nothing to look ahead to.'

In contrast, all of the others are lonely:

- Candy wants to join George and Lennie ''cause I ain't got no relatives nor nothing' and he soon 'won't have no place to go'. His only friend was his old dog, which is shot by Carlson.
- Crooks, although apparently protective of his own room – 'This here's my room. Nobody got any right in here but me' – does enjoy Lennie's visit: 'you might as well set down'. He talks about being lonely, and says: 'I tell ya a guy gets too lonely an' he gets sick.'
- Curley's wife is so desperate for company that she goes where she is not wanted on the ranch: 'Think I don't like to talk to somebody ever' once in a while?' She is the only woman on the ranch and her husband is fiercely jealous.

- Notice how desperate all of the characters are for someone to listen to them. Whit, for example, enjoys talking about the letter in the magazine, even though it means nothing to others. There are several one-sided conversations – it is having someone to talk to that is important. As Crooks says, 'a guy needs somebody – to be near him'.
- Loneliness leads Candy to offer his savings to George. It also leads Crooks to ask to join them.
- In what ways do you think loneliness affects Curley's behaviour?

## THE AMERICAN DREAM

Crooks says of the itinerant workers: 'they come, an' quit an' go on, an' every damn one of 'em's got a little piece of land in his head.' George and Lennie's dream is typical of what many aspire to, but the underlying feeling is that no one ever achieves it. Crooks is very cynical, as is George at the end – 'I think I knowed . . . we'd never do her. He usta like to hear about it so much I got to thinking maybe we would.' Yet he was hopeful after Candy's offered money.

Find the many references to dreams – particularly George and Lennie's – and keep notes to help you understand how important dreams and hopes are to all of the characters.

## PREJUDICE

There are many examples of prejudice in the novel:

- racism – consider the way Crooks is treated
- sexism – Curley's wife is ostracized by the men.

What other examples of prejudice can you find?

### ESSAY QUESTIONS: THEMES AND ISSUES

1 To what extent does prejudice affect the attitudes and behaviour of the characters?
2 Do you believe that all of the characters are lonely to some extent? Consider their words, actions, and relationships.

### EXAMINATION QUESTIONS

1 Who do you think is most to blame for Lennie's death?
2 Is Slim the only character who deserves your respect or do any of the others have admirable qualities?
3 Do you feel sympathy for any of the characters? Support your answer by referring to their words, actions, and behaviour.
4 Do you agree that the characters are more interesting than the events?

# LORD OF THE FLIES

## *William Golding*

> *Before beginning this unit, go back to pages 83–84 and read again what examiners are looking for in an essay about post-1914 prose.*

## BACKGROUND AND CONTEXT

*Lord of the Flies* was written in 1953 and set in the near future. Its background is the threat of atomic warfare after Word War Two, when dangerous differences arose between the East and West. Golding assumed that in the event of atomic war, there would be mass evacuation of children away from the northern hemisphere. His characters are stranded on the island because the boys survive when their plane crashes, and only the passenger tube lands safely.

One of the most important facts is that the boys are left without adult supervision. Although why and how they got there may not seem vital, we cannot ignore what is going on in the rest of the world, as the violence of the boys on the island is not unlike that of the so-called civilized world which is consumed by war. Golding gives us clues about this.

### RESEARCH ACTIVITY

Find the quotations in Chapter 1 to prove the following:
- Their plane was attacked.
- The rest of the plane, other than the passenger tube, came down in flames.
- The 'scar' was created by the passenger tube landing.
- They landed in a storm, which then dragged the tube out to sea.
- The pilot had said something about an atom bomb, and many people were probably dead.

We are occasionally reminded of the war that is raging in the rest of the world. In Chapter 1, Ralph pretends to be a fighter plane, and later, on the first exploration of the island, Ralph, Jack, and Simon push a rock over the edge, and it falls 'like a bomb.'

In Chapter 6, the 'battle fought at ten miles' height' results in the arrival of the dead parachutist.

In the closing pages, the boys come face to face with a naval officer, whose cutter is moored offshore and whose ratings each 'held a sub-machine gun.'

You must remember that the degeneration of the boys is played out against this backdrop of a warring society, one to which the boys will return. Even though they have been rescued from the island, they have not been rescued from fighting.

## SETTING

Near the beginning of Chapter 2, Ralph says, 'This is our island. It's a good island. Until the grown-ups come to fetch us we'll have fun.'

The island setting is important – if the boys had simply been able to walk inland, there would have been no problems and no story! The fact that they are on an island emphasizes their isolation from the rest of the world. They have to look after themselves. At first this seems good, but by the end the boys have ruined the island.

What do we find out about the setting in the opening chapter? Consider the following quotations from the first paragraph:
- 'the long scar smashed into the jungle'
- 'a bath of heat'
- 'creepers and broken trunks'
- 'vision of red and yellow'
- 'witch-like cry'.

Notice how you are given two contrasting pictures of the island. The use of words like 'scar', 'smashed', 'broken', and 'witch-like' suggests destruction. On the other hand, 'bath', 'heat', 'red', 'yellow' convey a sense of warmth and colour.

---

**▌WRITING ACTIVITY**

**1** Consider the following words, which appear over the next few pages:

| | | |
|---|---|---|
| jungle | reef | creeper things |
| lagoon | scratched by thorns | fruit |
| jagged end of a trunk | storm | dragged |
| tripped | disentangled | broken trunk |

Write down the ideas these words suggest to you about the island.

---

In spite of Ralph's excitement, there is an underlying feeling that the island is not a friendly, welcoming place.

The paragraph beginning 'The shore was fledged with palm trees' presents some sort of balance, as there is a sense of relaxation in the words 'leaned or reclined'. However, the same paragraph talks of 'coarse grass,' 'fallen trees', 'decaying coconuts', and the 'darkness of the forest'. There is further contrast with 'shimmering water', 'white surf flinked', 'still as a mountain lake', and 'blue of all shades and shadowy green and purple.'

The repetition of words like 'beach' and 'palm' creates a stereotypical vision of a tropical island which excites Ralph – and the reader. However, the reader must not forget the underlying sense of a threat, which is summarized in the next paragraph: 'the heat hit him'.

As the boys move around the island, so the reader is invited to follow and notice details such as 'Here the beach was interrupted abruptly'. The sense of space is clearly broken.

The description conveys a sense of colour, light, and movement, through words such as 'pink', 'green', 'reflections', 'efflorescence of tropical weed and coral', and 'glittering'.

In Ralph's eyes, this is a paradise island, but although we can share in Ralph's euphoria, we must not ignore Golding's warning about its dangers. The warning is present throughout Chapter 1, and becomes important later:

- the creepers in the trees start the rumours about a beast
- the heat affects the boys' behaviour and routine
- the next storm is particularly violent, and so is the boys' behaviour
- at the end, Ralph has to pick his way through the jungle.

## WRITING ACTIVITY

2 Towards the end of Chapter 1, Ralph, Jack, and Simon explore the island and climb the mountain. Find the paragraph beginning 'It was roughly boat-shaped'. Using this paragraph and any other information you can find, draw a map of the island and label the reef, the lagoon, the mountain, the platform, the jungle, the scar, the pool, the fort, and the criss-crossed trunks.

# CHARACTERS

Exam questions on characters could be based on one character:
*What makes Jack change from head choirboy to a savage?*
*To what extent do you consider Simon to be batty?*

They could also be comparative:
*Was Ralph a good leader? Would Jack have been a better one?*
*Which pair do you find more interesting – Jack and Roger or Ralph and Piggy?*

This section will show you how to collect information about key characters, and how to track their development and their relationships.

When characters are first introduced, we are often given straight-forward facts about them. For example, Ralph is introduced as 'the boy with fair hair', Jack is 'tall, thin, and bony'. We are also given clues about their personality. We are told about Ralph that 'there was a mildness about his mouth and eyes that proclaimed no devil'. This contrasts directly with Jack, whose 'light blue eyes' are 'ready to turn to anger'.

## CHARACTER TRACKING

It is important that you build up a detailed set of notes on the characters along with brief quotations as proof. We will begin by tracking Piggy in Chapter 1.

Look closely at the way Piggy is introduced in the opening pages:
- He is introduced anonymously as 'the voice'.
- He is wearing a 'greasy wind-breaker' and his knees are 'plump' and 'scratched'.
- He is compared to 'the fair boy' and is 'shorter . . . and very fat' and wears 'thick spectacles'.
- He speaks non-standard English when he talks of 'them fruit' and claims 'we was attacked!'
- He is desperate for friendship and recognition and so 'hung steadily at his shoulder' and tried to get 'the fair boy' to ask him his name.
- There is a sense of pride because of his disabilities: 'I was the only boy in our school what had asthma . . . And I've been wearing specs since I was three.'

- He is greedy and, on more than one occasion, 'crouched down among the tangled foliage' because he has eaten too much of 'them fruit'.
- He reluctantly divulges his nickname —'I don't care what they call me . . . so long as they don't call me what they used to call me at school.' His nickname 'Piggy' along with the other information marks him as the stereotypical bully's victim. This is emphasized by Ralph's reaction, which also creates a feeling of sympathy when 'Piggy grinned reluctantly, pleased despite himself at even this much recognition'.

## WRITING ACTIVITY

1 More information about Piggy is given in the rest of the chapter. Find the evidence for these points and decide what they tell you about Piggy:
- He is uneasy at the thought of there being no adults.
- When Ralph goes swimming, Piggy watches 'enviously'.
- He is unused to physical activity because of his asthma.
- He is an orphan brought up by an indulgent aunt who owned a sweet shop.
- He is mature and puts up with Ralph's teasing 'with a sort of humble patience'.
- He is observant – he knows the plane has gone down in flames and that the pilot must have been killed.
- He is logical: 'They're all dead . . . an' this is an island. Nobody don't know we're here.'
- He gives Ralph the credit for calling the meeting.
- He is immediately scared of Jack.
- He has a habit of cleaning his glasses when he is nervous or embarrassed.
- He believes he has a special relationship with Ralph.

Jack arrives in response to the sound of the conch. He leads his choir along the beach, and expects to find adults organizing them. We are given the following facts:

- He is 'tall, thin, and bony'.
- His hair is red.
- He is 'freckled' and 'ugly'.
- His eyes are 'light blue' and staring.
- He is head boy, chapter chorister, and can sing C sharp.

## WRITING ACTIVITIES

2 Find the evidence for the following character traits in Jack:
- He is bossy.
- He is aggressive.
- He is unsympathetic and intimidating.
- He is a bully.
- He cannot accept failure.

3 Now do the same for Ralph, beginning with the facts, then looking for information about his personality.

As you read through the novel build up detailed character logs on all of the main characters, keeping note of information and what it tells you about them. Notice also how they change, and look for any clues that may prepare us for what they do.

**ESSAY QUESTION: CHARACTERS**

What do we learn about Ralph, Jack, and Piggy in the first chapter?

## PLOT AND STRUCTURE

The novel follows the boys during their time on the island, from their first meeting to their rescue.

### CHAPTER 1 *The Sound of the Shell*

This chapter brings the boys together – first Ralph and Piggy, who discover the conch and use it to call the other boys, including Jack and the choir, to the beach. When they realize there are no adults and so they must look after themselves, they elect Ralph as their leader. Ralph chooses Jack and Simon to help him explore. They discover that they are on an uninhabited island.

**WRITING ACTIVITIES**

1 Was Ralph the best choice of leader? Why was he chosen? Would you have voted for him? Why, or why not?
2 Was Ralph right to offer Jack control of the choir? Why, or why not?
3 Do you agree with Ralph's choice of Jack and Simon? Why, or why not?
4 Look for detail about the friendship between the boys. Does anything make you feel uneasy?

### CHAPTER 2 *Fire on the Mountain*

Ralph explains to the assembled boys that they are on an uninhabited island – a 'good island' that will provide them with everything they need until they are rescued. The idea of a 'beastie' is first suggested by the boy with the birthmark. Ralph's attempt to convince them that the island is too small for a beast is undermined by Jack who says he and his hunters will search to make sure. There is now a shadow of doubt over the island. The focus returns to the idea of rescue and Ralph suggests the need for a signal fire. The boys rush to the top of the mountain, much to Piggy's disgust, and build a huge fire which they light with Piggy's glasses. Unfortunately, the fire spreads out of control – and the boy with the birthmark is apparently killed.

▮ **WRITING ACTIVITIES**

1 How do the conch, the fire, and Piggy's glasses acquire a level of importance?
2 What does Piggy's comment 'Acting like a crowd of kids' add to your understanding of his personality?
3 What evidence is there in this chapter to suggest Ralph's simple trust in adults?
4 Look carefully at the paragraph beginning 'Smoke was rising here and there'. Consider the imagery – Golding's use of similes, metaphors, and alliteration.

## CHAPTER 3 *Huts on the Beach*

Jack becomes obsessed with hunting and killing a pig and has learnt how to track. Ralph, however, is becoming more and more frustrated at their clumsy attempts to build shelters and the lack of help. There is some antagonism when Ralph and Jack reveal different priorities – Ralph wants rescue, whereas Jack wants to hunt and kill. Meanwhile, Simon goes off alone to a secret place he has found, and crawls under 'a great mat' to hide.

▮ **WRITING ACTIVITIES**

1 Find references to Jack's eyes and examples of animal imagery. What do these add to your understanding of him?
2 Find the points where Ralph and Jack are friends, and then where they fall out. What causes their disagreements?
3 Why do you think Simon behaves in the way he does?

## CHAPTER 4 *Painted Faces and Long Hair*

The boys adapt to life on the island and the 'littluns', who have no real understanding of what is going on, are able to keep themselves amused. Henry, Percival, and Johnny are playing on the beach when Roger, followed by Maurice, destroys the sandcastles. Maurice feels guilty when he gets sand in Percival's eyes and goes off. Roger hides to watch Henry and throws stones at him – but aims to miss.

Jack has decided to paint his face so the pigs cannot see him. He creates an horrific mask behind which he can hide and be 'liberated from shame and self-consciousness'. He leads his hunters off on a chase. Meanwhile, Ralph and Piggy are discussing rescue when Ralph sees smoke from a ship's funnel on the horizon. They panic because they have no signal. They rush to the top of the mountain – there are no hunters and no fire.

When Jack and his hunters appear they are carrying a dead pig and chanting. They want to share the excitement of the kill, but quickly realize that something is wrong. Jack knows he is at fault but when Piggy complains, Jack retaliates by hitting Piggy and breaking his glasses. He apologizes for letting the fire go out. The boys enjoy a feast, although Jack tries to keep Piggy out. The hunters relive the kill with Maurice pretending to be the pig until Ralph calls a meeting.

## ▌WRITING ACTIVITIES

1 In your own words, describe how the 'littluns' spend their time.
2 Look carefully at the description of Roger and what he does. What can you deduce about him?
3 Maurice feels guilty and Roger throws to miss – explain the significance of these facts.
4 What do Johnny and Henry 'learn' from Maurice?
5 Consider the behaviour of Ralph and Jack in this chapter – who appears to have the strongest leadership qualities? Note your evidence and reasons.
6 What is your opinion of Jack's treatment of Piggy? Why do you think he hates Piggy so much?

## CHAPTER 5 *Beast from Water*

Ralph is beginning to understand the seriousness of their situation. The mood is very solemn. Ralph talks about their rules and insists that they obey them. He introduces a new rule – they will only have fire on the mountain. He reminds them of the importance of fire and rescue, before inviting discussion about fear. Jack has been everywhere on the island and found no evidence of a real beast – it must therefore be intangible. The discussion moves from the fear of people, to giant squids, to ghosts. The majority vote to say they believe in ghosts. Jack shows his contempt for Ralph and the conch and leaves the assembly. Ralph considers giving up the leadership, but is persuaded not to by Piggy and Simon.

## ▌WRITING ACTIVITIES

1 Look at the way Ralph behaves and the things he says and does in this chapter – do you think he has acted wisely? Give your reasons. Should he give up the leadership? Why, or why not?
2 What rules have the boys made? Why do you think they are unable to keep them?
3 Look carefully at the way Golding builds the atmosphere and note effective examples of descriptive detail.

4  What does Jack's behaviour add to your understanding of him?

5  Note what Simon says and does, and add to your character log.

## CHAPTER 6 *Beast from Air*

While the boys sleep restlessly, they are unaware of the battle being fought in the air, which results in a dead parachutist landing on the mountain near the fire. Samneric are on duty at the fire, but have both fallen asleep. When they wake, they check the fire before noticing there is no longer a gap between the rocks. They rush to the beach and tell of a ferocious beast that chased them. The 'biguns' set off on a real hunt, though Jack is annoyed that Piggy stays to look after the 'littluns'. They search the end of the island, which Jack decides would be a good place for a fort.

### ▌WRITING ACTIVITIES

1  How are we reminded of what is going on in the rest of the world?

2  Why is it ironic that the parachutist lands this particular night? (You may want to look at the end of Chapter 5.)

3  To what extent do Samneric exaggerate what they have seen?

4  How does Ralph assert his leadership?

5  What do you understand to be Ralph's 'personal hell'?

## CHAPTER 7 *Shadows and Tall Trees*

The boys' search is interrupted by the chase of a pig. Ralph shares in the excitement and enjoys the hunt. They enact killing a pig, with Robert pretending to be the pig, until they really hurt him. Simon goes to tell Piggy they won't be back yet and the rest continue the search for the beast. There is a great deal of antagonism between Ralph and Jack. On top of the mountain, Ralph, Jack, and Roger see 'a figure that bulged' and rush back to the beach.

### ▌WRITING ACTIVITIES

1  Why do you think Ralph enjoys the chase?

2  Why should we be concerned about the 'game' in which Robert is hurt?

3  Consider what Simon says and does, and what it adds to your understanding of him.

4  Examine the relationship between Ralph and Jack. Does Jack hate Ralph?

5  What is the significance of Ralph's daydreaming and the emphasis on the boys' dirtiness?

## CHAPTER 8 *Gift for the Darkness*

Jack calls a meeting, argues with Ralph and calls for a vote. The boys want Ralph to stay as chief, so Jack leaves, saying he's 'not going to play any longer'. Simon suggests climbing the mountain. Piggy suggests building a fire on the beach. It is good for them to be busy, but they do not notice that many boys have followed Jack.

A euphoric Jack leads a successful hunt in which their victim is a sow that is feeding piglets. They plan to steal fire from Ralph's group and leave the pig's head on a stick as a gift for the beast. Simon later sees this head and it seems to speak to him.

As a storm begins to build, Ralph and Piggy try to understand what has gone wrong. Jack and his tribe steal fire and Jack invites them all to a feast. Piggy thinks they have come for the conch. Ralph struggles to explain the importance of fire and rescue. Simon, alone with the pig's head, appears to have a fit.

### ▌WRITING ACTIVITIES

1 Simon behaves strangely here. Track what he says and does and look for clues about his health. What do you make of his conversation with the pig's head?
2 Note what Jack says and does, particularly what he says about Ralph, his reaction to losing the vote, his choice of the sow, his theft and invitation.
3 What evidence is there that Ralph is finding it harder to keep a clear head?
4 Find references to the coming storm and comment on Golding's imagery.

## CHAPTER 9 *A View to a Death*

The parallel narrative in this chapter helps us to see what is happening at different places at the same time. Simon recovers and finds out exactly what the beast is. He wants to let the others know that it is harmless. Ralph and Piggy are bathing to try to keep cool as the storm builds. They decide to go to Jack's 'party' to make sure nothing goes wrong. Jack sits apart from the boys 'like an idol'. He confidently gives orders and invites boys to join his tribe, ignoring Ralph's interruptions. When Ralph mentions the coming storm and the need for shelters, Jack distracts the boys by calling for them to do their dance. They become more and more hysterical; the noise is intensified by the thunder and lightning. As they look for a boy to play the part of the pig, Simon crawls out of the forest, but is not recognized. The boys pounce on him and kill him. Once the dance is over, the storm dies away, and Simon's body is washed out to sea. Ironically, the parachutist's body is also carried away in the storm.

## WRITING ACTIVITIES

1 Do you think the structure of this chapter is helpful?
2 Look closely at the opening paragraphs about Simon. Examine the language and imagery, and the way the atmosphere becomes ominous. Is it effective?
3 Do you notice any change in Piggy's behaviour?
4 What is your opinion of Jack's style of leadership? Is he a better leader than Ralph? Look carefully at what he says.
5 Examine how Golding intensifies the atmosphere, building up to the horrific detail of Simon's death. Look carefully at vocabulary, imagery, and sentence structure. Then compare the style and tone of the last three paragraphs.

## CHAPTER 10 *The Shell and the Glasses*

The next morning, only Ralph, Piggy, and Samneric are left. They find it hard to talk about what happened. Meanwhile, Jack has set up camp on the end of the island. He is a vicious leader. He denies that they killed the beast and again plans to raid the others for fire. It is a struggle for Ralph and the other three to keep the fire going so they decide to let it go out until morning. Ralph dreams of home. They are raided by Jack and two others, who easily escape with Piggy's glasses while they fight each other in the darkness and confusion.

## WRITING ACTIVITIES

1 Compare the four boys' reactions to events of the previous night.
2 Examine Jack's style of leadership and the orders he gives. Why do you think they say he's 'a proper chief'?
3 Examine what the boys say and do, and how the atmosphere changes as the narrative moves towards the raid.
4 How can we tell the four boys in the shelter fight each other?

## CHAPTER 11 *Castle Rock*

Piggy insists that they demand the return of his glasses and they discuss how best to do this, knowing that Jack and his tribe will be savages hiding behind masks. They approach Jack's fort, and Piggy kneels, cradling the conch, while Ralph tries to reason with Jack. Jack is annoyed at being called a thief, and he and Ralph fight. Samneric are taken prisoner. Piggy shouts at the boys, while Roger throws stones at Ralph. He then leans on a lever, causing a rock to roll down the mountain and knock Piggy onto the rocks. The fall kills him and destroys the conch. Ralph runs away.

## WRITING ACTIVITIES

1  How and why do the four boys try to make themselves look civilized?
2  Compare the procession of the four boys with that of the choir in the first chapter.
3  Do you think Ralph handles the confrontation effectively? Why, or why not? Look closely at what he says.
4  Why does Jack react so angrily to being called a thief?
5  What is symbolic about the breaking of the conch?
6  What is your opinion of Roger and what he does?

## CHAPTER 12 *Cry of the Hunters*

Ralph hopes they will leave him alone. He goes off to find food, comes across the pig's skull and destroys it. Returning to hide near the Castle Rock, he realizes they are holding a feast. Samneric are on watch. They give Ralph some meat, but warn him that he is going to be hunted the next day. Roger has sharpened a stick at both ends. Ralph makes the mistake of saying where he will hide. Samneric are tortured to make them tell.

The next morning, Ralph hears the ululation of the savages, and only just manages to escape from his hiding place before a rock lands on it. Jack decides to smoke Ralph out of wherever he tries to hide. With the island on fire, and Ralph running out of hiding places and energy, he collapses onto the beach – at the feet of a naval officer who says they have seen the smoke and assumes the boys are playing. Jack does not disagree when Ralph says he is chief. Percival's attempt to identify himself fails. Ralph finally breaks down.

## WRITING ACTIVITIES

1  Why is Ralph unable to recognize most of the boys?
2  Look at the two pages following the sentence 'When he had eaten he went towards the beach'. Examine the imagery, particularly Golding's use of alliteration. What effect does this have?
3  What is the significance of the stick sharpened at both ends?
4  What options does Ralph have during the chase? What would you have done?
5  What is the significance of Percival's loss of memory?
6  Why does Jack not dispute Ralph's claim to be the leader?
7  Why must the novel end with rescue?

## THEMES AND ISSUES

What is *Lord of the Flies* all about?

In 1993, following the murder of James Bulger, Golding wrote: 'It was nearly 40 years ago that I wrote about the cruelty boys can inflict on each other . . . Are men and women born with cruelty as a deep component of their nature? Is civilisation largely an heroic struggle to build layer upon layer upon the rough and splintered raw material of humankind? Or does it make a truer picture if we imagine the new-born child as a blank slate upon which the harshness of experience prints its indelible and frightening patterns? . . . There are . . . conditions in which cruelty seems to flourish . . . chaos is one, fear is another.'

*The Daily Mail*, Wednesday 17 February 1993

*Lord of the Flies* was written in response to R. M. Ballantyne's 1858 novel *The Coral Island*, in which a group of boys was stranded on a desert island. Set against a background of Victorian optimism and British imperialism, the novel shows the boys working together bravely and unselfishly, and they remain completely civilized until their rescue. In contrast, Golding's novel is set against a background of post-war pessimism and the boys are greedy, selfish, and afraid.

Golding presents the reader with contrasting characters who all represent different levels of evil. At one end of the scale is Roger, who at first throws stones at Henry intending to miss, then deliberately causes the rock to roll and kill Piggy. He becomes the sadistic torturer, with the 'hangman's horror' clinging to him. Johnny learns how to make Percival cry and Henry becomes 'absorbed beyond mere happiness as he felt himself exercising control over living things'. Even Ralph is carried away with the excitement of the hunt 'and felt that hunting was good after all'. He becomes as desperate as Roger to stab at Robert as 'the desire to squeeze and hurt was over-mastering'. Piggy is present at Simon's murder. Golding shows how Jack changes from a bossy choir leader into a cruel tyrant who orders Ralph's death.

Only Simon is never tainted by evil – he is consistently helpful and unselfish. He helps to build the huts, he picks fruit for the 'littluns', he is kind to Piggy when his glasses are broken, he crosses the island alone at night to help Piggy, and he climbs the mountain to discover the truth about the beast. He does not give in to fear – and fear is one of Golding's conditions in which cruelty flourishes. Simon understands that the beast is 'only us', yet he is killed when he tries to tell the others. Here, evil triumphs over goodness.

In the end, it is only the arrival of the naval officer that stops evil from triumphing over goodness again by killing Ralph.

### WRITING ACTIVITY

1 Golding believed that fear was a necessary condition for cruelty to flourish – and the boys are certainly afraid. Make notes about what they are afraid of, from the dark to Ralph's final fear of being caught. Consider how they cope with this emotion.

The conch becomes a powerful symbol of law and order, free speech, democracy, and unity. It is the conch that first brings the boys together; it is the main reason for Ralph being elected leader and helps him to control the meetings. It is significant that the conch is destroyed when Piggy is killed.

### WRITING ACTIVITY

2 Find references to the conch and make notes about how it is described.

Piggy's glasses, fire, and the pig's head are also symbols. The boys cannot light the fire without the glasses, and without fire they cannot be rescued or cook the meat from the pigs they kill. Ironically, fire kills one boy and nearly destroys Ralph – yet it does lead to their rescue. The glasses therefore symbolize life and death.

### WRITING ACTIVITIES

3 Investigate Golding's use of symbolism, finding information to demonstrate the significance of the conch, glasses, and fire, and by considering the importance of the beast and the pig's head.

4 Select two or three characters. Under the headings 'good' and 'evil' list their words, actions, and character traits. Use your findings to decide which is dominant – good or evil. You may like to present your work in the form of spider diagrams. For example, you could use the diagram on page 147 as a starting point.

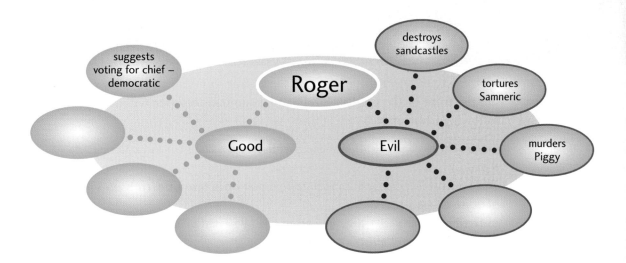

Roger

destroys sandcastles

tortures Samneric

murders Piggy

suggests voting for chief – democratic

Good

Evil

EXAMINATION QUESTIONS

1 Compare the leadership styles of Ralph and Jack, examining the personality traits that affect their leadership style.

2 The Lord of the Flies tells Simon 'they think you're batty'. Do you agree that Simon is 'batty'? Examine his personality and behaviour, and his attempts to explain what is going on.

3 Which pair do you find more interesting – Ralph and Piggy or Jack and Roger? Justify your answer by considering what they say and do.

4 Examine the importance of the conch, fire, Piggy's glasses, and the pig's head on a stick. To what extent are these symbolic?

5 How far do you agree that it was inevitable that the boys would break into two opposing groups? You need to consider the characters involved and their reactions to different situations.

6 How are the boys changed by their experiences on the island? Look closely at any two of the boys.

7 Do you agree that the boys changed the island from paradise to hell?

8 Examine Golding's use of imagery and comment on its effectiveness. You could look in particular at the descriptions of the fires, the storm, and the hunts.

9 Do the boys bring evil to the island, or does the island exert an evil influence on them?

10 What do you consider to be the main message of the novel?

# How you will be assessed

On the front of the English Literature examination paper will be the following instructions:

*Answer **three** questions. Answer one question from each of the three Sections: A, B and C.*
*There are two questions set on each text. Answer **only one question on each of your chosen texts**.*
*In Section B some poetry texts are set for pre-1914 and some for post-1914. Check your choice of questions carefully.*

Section A will be the Drama questions, Section B Poetry, Section C Prose. You can answer the three questions **in any order**, but make sure you number the answers clearly.

Your three examination answers will be assessed against four objectives:

1 How you respond to the texts you have studied. This includes how well you show you understand the texts and support your comments with brief textual evidence.
2 How you explore the ways writers use language and structure their texts. You may discuss any different ways texts can be interpreted by the reader.
3 In poetry: your understanding of the comparisons or contrasts between poems, supporting your comments with brief references to the poems.
4 In the drama answers particularly: your understanding of context and the importance of the background against which the text was written.

In every examination the top marks are awarded to candidates who **focus** on the details of the question. Their comments show their critical **understanding** of the text, and their **appreciation** of the writer's use of language. They support their commentary with **brief textual references**.

Each question will carry equal marks. **Each** of your answers will be about 23% of the total for the whole GCSE (and that includes coursework). **Each** examination answer is worth just over twice what each coursework assignment is worth. Up to three marks in both the written examination and coursework are awarded for your 'Quality of Written Communication'.

You will be entered for one of the following two tiers:

- Foundation Tier (Tier F), with the highest grade being a C and the lowest pass grade a G
- Higher Tier (Tier H) with the highest grade being A* and the lowest grade a D.

Although you will be able to study the same texts, the questions will be slightly harder at Tier H. At Tier F, bullet points will help to guide candidates.

The examiner marking your answers will be given clear instructions from the Chief Examiner about what to look for in candidates' answers. After each year's examination has finished, the Chief Examiner writes a report which tells the teachers preparing candidates for the examination the main mistakes that candidates tend to make. If you know what these mistakes are, you can avoid losing marks in that way and gain the highest marks your answers deserve.

For example, examiners say many candidates produce their weakest and shortest answers in the poetry section. The main weakness is they do not look closely enough at the poet's use of language. They identify rhyme, metaphor, simile, onomatopoeia, and personification, but do not discuss how the poet uses these for effect. Examiners report that the best poetry answers show not only close knowledge of the poem, but make interesting points about the ideas and the poet's use of language.

Examiners assessing your answers will reward what you write, not look for what is 'missing'. The main thing they assess is the quality of the comments that show knowledge, understanding, and insight. They reward most highly those answers that keep the question firmly in mind, and offer textual evidence in support of points being made. Above all, they will reward an answer that shows a personal response coming from a thoughtful engagement with the text.

# PREPARING FOR THE EXAMINATION

## PLANNING

You need to plan your time carefully leading up to the examinations, with some kind of timetable or calendar to fit in all the revision demands of the different subjects.

### REVISION

The activities you have worked through in this *Students' Book* will have prepared you for the written examination. What you have to do now is put all that preparation into some order so you can revise it.

In the written examination you will have a choice of questions on the three texts you have studied. This book will have helped you put together a set of notes for each of the texts. The examination will allow you about 40 minutes to answer each question, so you have to see if you can turn your notes and plans into 40-minute answers.

Take your notes on the different aspects of each text and write them out on A4 paper in an easy-to-remember style. You could use different-coloured pens, or underline key words, or you could use different-shaped spaces on your paper to help you remember.

To improve your performance in examination conditions, follow this advice: After revising your notes on one of the texts, put them away and write a timed answer in 40 minutes to a question of your choice. It could be one that is given in this book.

When you have finished your answer, check it against your notes to see what you remembered correctly and what you need to improve.

The next step is to answer an 'unseen' question in 40 minutes. Ask your teacher to set you the question. This exercise is best done under supervision in 'exam conditions'. After your teacher has marked it, check it for what you remembered and what you need to improve.

When you have written several answers on each text, you can turn your notes into **revision cards** which have only the **key words** or ideas for each of the main areas of revision. For example, for poetry you might have key words on theme and subject matter, language and imagery, tone, structure and form, and links for comparison with other poems. Make a card for each poem you have studied in depth in preparation for the examination.

Remember that the Chief Examiner has written the questions to find out what you know, understand, and appreciate about the texts you have studied. The questions are not traps set for you. If you have carefully studied the texts, considered the writers' intentions, and understood how the language and structure have helped their meaning, you will find that both questions will give you scope to show your knowledge, understanding, and appreciation.

# THE BIG DAY

Avoid last-minute revision, whatever your friends or classmates seem to be doing or saying. Last-minute revision is the lottery approach to passing exams! Be prepared, confident, and as relaxed as possible. Make sure you have your copies of the texts (from 2005 these must be without notes), your watch, a highlighter pen and two good quality black or dark blue pens. Don't be tempted to lend one of your pens to someone who has arrived unprepared. Any pen might stop working in the examination room and you need a spare.

## IN THE EXAMINATION

**Read the front of the paper carefully**. The instructions are called the **rubric**, and they are vitally important. The rubric tells you all you need to know about how to complete the examination. Use your highlighter pen to mark the key words of the rubric.

Then, turn to the page with the questions on your text. **Double check** that it is your text and not a similar one, such as the two sections of *Best Words*.

**Read both questions carefully** and then use your highlighter again to pick out the key words. These are very important – many candidates rush and misread the instructions. The instructions for answering the question are contained in words such as *compare two scenes* or *theme of loneliness* or *at least one other poem* or *the concluding chapter* or *the important features of your chosen characters*. Reading these instructions carefully will ensure you don't lose marks by answering only part of the question – or in some cases the wrong question altogether.

Now **focus** on the key words of the question you have chosen to answer. Jot down an outline plan of your answer, using your recall of the notes you wrote on your revision cards. You should spend about five minutes on this planning stage. Don't be tempted to rush into your answer. The planning will allow you time to think through your approach to the question.

Now begin writing. Make sure that in your first paragraph you give a clear answer to the question. Then develop a well-organized answer bringing in whatever points you think are valid. Keep the question in focus and make at least one other clear reference to it in your answer – such as *'Another feature of Heaney's appeal to the senses is found in his frequent use of onomatopoeia in both poems, such as . . .'*. You will have your texts with you, so don't be tempted to spend a lot of time writing out quotations. These should be brief and closely linked to the points you are making, and you should use them as **brief textual evidence** supporting your comments about areas such as *language* or *imagery* or *theme* or *characterization* or *structure*.

Avoid re-telling the story or main plot, especially in your drama and prose answers. You don't need to tell your examiner everything you know about the plot. What the examiner wants to know is if you can **select** important details or incidents. If you are answering, for example, on how Lennie's love of soft things gets him into trouble in *Of Mice and Men*, don't give long narrative accounts of the various episodes, such as the puppies or the incident in the barn. Instead select key details from these episodes to support the points you are making.

In your final paragraph, go back to the **key words** of the question and **repeat** them in you concluding comments. *'Finally, in my opinion, these two poems best show how the writers have used their imaginations to explore the theme of love.'*

Make sure you do not spend much more than the allocated time for each answer. You will score badly if you leave an answer unfinished. As a rough guide, two excellent answers and one short, unfinished answer will not score as highly as three completed, good quality ones.

Remember that if you have prepared well, 40 minutes is not enough time to write everything you know about the text. Make sure you focus on the key details of the question and present your view on the topic you are asked about. The examiners are instructed to accept any approach to the texts as long as it is supported by textual evidence.

If there is time, go back and re-read each answer and check you have not made any errors due to slips of the pen.

## AFTERWARDS

When the examination is over, forget about it. Get on with revising for your next one. If you have prepared well and answered the three questions with a clear focus and detailed comments, supported with brief evidence from the text, then you will find you have done well when results day arrives!

The section 'How you will be assessed' (see page 148) told you that:

- The top marks are awarded to candidates who **focus** on the details of the question.
- Their comments show their critical **understanding** of the text and **appreciation** of the writer's use of language.
- They support their commentary with **brief textual references**.

As a guide to the length of essays, something in the range of 250–400 words is expected, but this is only a very rough guide, as **quality** is far more important than quantity, and you need to develop your points to get high grades. Of course, clear and concise essays will score higher marks than long, rambling ones.

Here are some extracts from examination answers with comments from senior examiners. From studying these extracts and comments, you will see the skills that you need to show in your own answers.

1 First is a Tier F candidate answering a question on *An Inspector Calls*, asking which character learns most about the social conditions of the working class from the way Eva Smith was treated. The candidate begins the answer like this:

*'An Inspector Calls' is an interesting play of a young working-class girl who needs help with her life but none of them continues to help her the best they can and so each one suffers the consequences. But none of them realize what they have done until it is too late.*

*The play starts off with the Birling family having a party. Mr Birling owns a company; he and his wife have two children Eric and Sheila. She is engaged to Gerald Croft. They are all middle class. An Inspector calls and interrupts their celebration.*

## EXAMINER'S COMMENTS

Marks would be awarded for the valid knowledge. However, in the opening paragraph there is no explicit focus on the question. *'Which character?'* are key words which need to be addressed early in the answer. The opening paragraph also lacks clear expression; does 'none of them' refer to all of the other characters, apart from the Inspector?

The second paragraph makes the mistake of beginning a narrative account of the play. This has some value, but the danger lies in including everything and not selecting key incidents. The candidate, not the examiner, must pick out what is directly relevant to the question. This answer, if developed along the same lines, would probably achieve a mark in the grade D range. It shows knowledge, but does not select the key events nor focus on one character.

The opening would have been improved by this approach:

'An Inspector Calls' is an interesting play about a young working-class girl who needs help with her life. None of the middle-class characters really help her the best they can and in the end each one suffers the consequences of their behaviour. In my opinion Sheila is the character who learns most about the harsh conditions of working-class life from Eva's experiences. But even she realizes too late to help Eva.

In the opening scene we meet Sheila as her wealthy family is celebrating her engagement to Gerald Croft. At this time Sheila seems to have no worries, but it all begins to change with the arrival of the Inspector.

2  Below is a Tier F candidate's answer on *Best Words*. The question asked for a comparison between two poems from the pre-1914 selection that have the theme of love. Here is the opening paragraph:

'First Love' is a good poem about a man who is experiencing love for the first time. It is a poem filled with senses and emotions. The poem begins with John Clare explaining the seasons. The first verse it is like spring, sudden and sweet. The second verse is as if he is talking about summer. It's hot and he's in love. The last is like winter and he's cold inside. The first two lines in the last verse are rhetorical questions.

## EXAMINER'S COMMENTS

The answer has several creditable points to make, but they are not at all developed or supported with textual references. There is no clear answer to the question's key words, *'compare two poems'*. There is a thin attempt to analyse the structure of the poem, with references to the theme of the seasons. The candidate does not make a good case as to why the first verse is spring and the second summer, but there would be some credit in this valid personal response.

The answer would be improved by clearly focusing on the question and using brief textual references to support the commentary. Here is how this opening could be improved to approach a C grade:

The two poems that I think best show how the theme of love is explored are 'First Love' and 'Ballad'. Both deal with the pain of love and both are about inexperience and naivety. Both use the idea of the seasons to explore the feelings of the people in love. 'First Love' is a good poem about a man who is experiencing love for the first time. It is a poem filled with appeals to the senses and powerful emotions.

The first verse of Clare's poem describes love as being 'sudden and so sweet'. 'Sweet' is repeated in the next line when he describes his love's face as like a 'sweet flower'. This is one of many natural images.

In the second verse he repeats how 'blood burnt' and 'blood rushed'. This makes me think this is like midsummer with all the heat. It also contrasts with the idea of winter in the final stanza. In this, Clare uses rhetorical questions in the first two lines to ask about winter and snow. This idea of the contrast between summer and winter is also used in 'Ballad'.

---

**3** This is a complete Tier H answer on *Of Mice and Men*, to a question asking which elements in the novel contribute to its success.

'Of Mice and Men' is a very popular novel telling the story of two guys looking out for each other and working on a ranch. The novel follows them and their friendship. In this essay I will show why the book is such a success by the friendship between Lennie and George and the setting and themes of the novel.

The two men in the novel are George and Lennie. George is small and witty, Lennie is large and simple. They are a complete contrast. This makes their friendship special. They are almost no way alike and don't share any interests. George promised to look after Lennie after his Aunt Clara died. It is however more of a friendship than just George looking after Lennie. In some ways Lennie is a pet to George. Lennie does what George says. He is also compared to an animal in 'big paws' and 'snorting like a horse'.

The themes of this novel are of authority, violence, and dreams. George and Lennie's friendship has all three of these. George is authoritative over Lennie, he gets angry and uses violence to get his authority, and together they have a dream, to 'live off the fatta the land'.

At the end their friendship is ended as George is caught up in the violence around him. Lennie has become a liability and also he isn't needed. The book is about getting rid of things that aren't needed, such as Candy's dog, Curley's wife, and Lennie. I think the ending helps its success as people see that friendship can last and can be formed by anyone. George doesn't want to kill Lennie but he has to, for Lennie's sake.

Finally I think its success is due to the long-lasting friendship of George and Lennie. Even through thick or thin they stay together and it is their two contrasting qualities that help them survive.

EXAMINER'S COMMENTS

The answer is of reasonable length, and it does attempt to answer the question in both the introduction and conclusion. It has valid knowledge of the text shown by a few brief close references, and some understanding of the issues that the novel explores. It sets out a clear structure but does not follow it, missing out a comment on the setting. Its main weakness, however, is that it touches on key points but does not explore them fully. This answer shows the candidate's potential for a grade C but it would probably be awarded a D.

4  Here is an extract from a poetry answer from a Tier H candidate. It is comparing how childhood memories are evoked in poetry.

In Heaney's two poems 'Churning Day' and 'An Advancement of Learning', there are many associated themes but I am concentrating on how he evokes childhood memories using appeals to the senses. In 'Churning Day' the memories are happy ones. The poem is about a day when all the family are churning milk to create butter. This is in contrast to 'An Advancement of Learning', where the memories are not so pleasant. This poem is about Heaney as a child walking along the embankment and facing two rats and eventually overcoming his fear. At the time of writing the poems the troubles in Northern Ireland were beginning to show and there are hints of this in some of Heaney's choice of words such as 'bombs' in 'Churning Day' and the references to battles in 'An Advancement of Learning', such as 'bridgehead', 'trained on me', and 'retreat'.

Both poems show how Heaney uses the senses to convey his memories of childhood. The fear in 'An Advancement of Learning' comes alive in the use of 'slimed' to describe the rat coming out of the water. The 's' sound in 'slimed' is close to other 's' sounds in 'Something slobbered' and 'smudging the silence'. All these 's' sounds create the slimy effect that the wet coat of the rat would have to look at and perhaps to touch.

EXAMINER'S COMMENTS

The candidate is covering all the main assessment points:

- a clear introduction answers the question
- the details of comparison between the poems show an understanding of Heaney's intentions
- there is detailed appreciation of the poet's use of language.

This essay, if continued using the same approach and quality, would achieve marks in the higher A*–C range.